# Texas and Worll

# TEXAS AND
# WORLD WAR I

*Gregory W. Ball*

Texas State Historical Association
Austin

Number 26 in the Fred Rider Cotten Popular History Series.
Cover image from Library of Congress, Prints and Photographs Division, https://www.loc.gov/resource/ppmsca.39708/ [Accessed July 10, 2018].

Library of Congress Cataloging-in-Publication Data

Names: Ball, Gregory W., 1969– author.
Title: Texas and World War I / Gregory W. Ball.
Other titles: Fred Rider Cotten popular history series ; no. 26.
Description: Austin : Texas State Historical Association, [2018] | Series:
    Number 26 in the Fred Rider Cotten popular history series
Identifiers: LCCN 2018016218 | ISBN 9781625110503
Subjects: LCSH: World War, 1914–1918—Texas. | World War, 1914–1918—Social
    aspects—Texas. | Texas—Politics and government—1865–1950.
Classification: LCC D570.85.T4 B35 2018 | DDC 940.3/764—dc23 LC record
available at https://lccn.loc.gov/2018016218

# CONTENTS

*Illustrations follow page 59*

# Acknowledgments

I would like to thank the Texas State Historical Association and the Texas Military Forces Museum for their support of this project. I would also like to thank Dr. Randolph B. Campbell, a great mentor and friend; Mr. Ryan Schumacher, editor, who went above and beyond in his support of this project; and Dr. Nicholas K. Roland, who helped edit the manuscript. Finally, thanks to my wife Sarah for her support and for simply being there. This work is dedicated to my mom, Carol C. Ball, who we lost too soon.

*Chapter 1*

# ORIGINS

World War I was truly a transformative event—not only on a global and national scale, but for Texas as well. As historian Walter Buenger has observed, what became known as the "Great War" forced many Texans to think like Americans rather than simply as Texans. Indeed, for Texas the era represents a transition from the trends of the nineteenth century to those of the twentieth, from the old to the new. Furthermore, many of the issues Texans confronted during World War I, such as border security, the status of foreign nationals within the country, the role of the military, and the political and social standing of women and minorities, echo to the present day.[1]

This study explores the contributions of Texans, elected leaders and everyday people alike, to the United States' effort in World War I. It examines how Texans prepared for the war, the role of the state in training soldiers and sailors for the war, the service of the nearly 200,000 Texans who served in the military during the war, and finally, the legacy of how World War I shaped Texas. This book begins with a brief exploration of the outbreak of conflict in 1914 and why the United States chose to intervene in the war in 1917. Other sections examine how Texans responded to President Woodrow Wilson's call for a declaration of war against Germany, including the state's congressional delegation, political leaders, and residents. Further sections explore the efforts to raise an army for service in France as well as the development of military sites within the state. The later sections focus on the combat service of Texans, with emphasis on the two American Expeditionary Forces (AEF) divisions most closely associated with the state, the 36th and 90th Divisions. The final chapter explores the legacy of the war and how the "Great War" influenced Texas's change from a rural, agricultural society, to the heavily urbanized, industrial state it is today.[2]

World War I occurred during a period of American history generally referred to as the Progressive Era. During the late nineteenth and early twentieth centuries, political measures often combined moral imperatives and social reform; two prominent examples were national prohibition and the expansion of voting rights for women. The nation's entry into the conflict raised questions of how Texans and other Americans would live up to the ideals of the age. How could the nation claim to fight a war in Europe with the avowed purpose of advancing democracy but fail to allow women to vote in all elections? If the United States claimed to be fighting a war for democracy in other countries, how would that shape how it treated its own minorities? If African Americans and Hispanics fought for democracy in Europe, would their efforts yield the same rights for their own people within the United States? Such questions would not be fully answered during and immediately after the war, and they would remain relevant over the ensuing decades of the twentieth century.

In August 1914, long simmering conflicts between European powers boiled over to become the most destructive war the world had ever seen. The "Great War" changed the world's political landscape and cast a long shadow over the remainder of the century; indeed, many major events to follow had their roots in World War I. In addition to the death and destruction in Europe, the war touched the lives of millions of American citizens, even though the United States did not intervene until it had raged for more than two years. How could such a war, fought thousands of miles away, affect the Lone Star State and the lives of thousands of its residents? To begin to answer such a question requires a brief exploration of how the war began and why the United States intervened.

The origins of World War I are rooted in the shifting "balance of power" that occurred in Europe throughout the nineteenth century and into the twentieth. Longtime adversaries Great Britain and France strove to maintain their continental and worldwide influence against a newly united economic and industrial powerhouse in Germany, which also threatened the influence of the fading (but still formidable) powers of Austria-Hungary and Russia in Central and Eastern Europe. Germany was but the most obvious example of the rising tide of nationalism throughout the continent; in Austria-Hungary, especially, various ethnic groups, including the Serbs, sought to establish nation-states of their own. The powder keg of national and ethnic rivalries exploded in the summer of 1914. On June 28, a Serbian nationalist, Gavrilo Princip, assassinated Archduke Franz Ferdinand, the heir to the Austrian throne, during his visit to Sarajevo. One month after the archduke's assassination, Austria-Hungary declared war on Serbia, which spurred Russia to declare war on Austria-Hungary. Germany, allied with Austria-Hungary, then declared war on Russia. For a variety of reasons, including a 1907 alliance called the Triple Entente with Russia and Germany's occupation of Belgium, France and Great Britain soon committed to the conflict. By early August, the European continent was at war. While American political leaders expressed concern over the war, few believed in August 1914 that the United States would be drawn into the war, seemingly rooted as it was in faraway ethnic, nationalistic, and political conflicts, and President Woodrow Wilson's isolationism exemplified the country's desire to stay neutral. Few on either side of the Atlantic imagined that the war would drag on for four years.[3]

The war in Western Europe began as a series of flanking maneuvers, as the Germans on one side and the British and French on the other attempted to outmaneuver each other across northwestern France and Belgium. By the fall of 1914, such maneuvers came to an end, and the lines stabilized. This led to the creation of a massive trench system along what became known as the Western Front, which stretched from the Belgian coast to the borders of neutral Switzerland hundreds of miles to the southeast. But fighting was not limited to the Western Front, as battles raged in Greece, Italy, Eastern Europe, Turkey and the Middle East, and even in East Africa. The years 1914 to 1917 are filled with the names of battles that have become legendary in the annals of military history: the Somme, Ypres, Passchendaele, Soissons, the Marne, Vimy, Verdun, and others too numerous to list.

The United States government faced many serious questions upon the outbreak of war in Europe. Could the nation remain neutral? Should the country become involved, and if so, which side should the U.S. support? How would the nation protect its right to free trade and the use of international waters? But rather than taking a side in the conflict, the United States began what has come to be known as the Preparedness Movement, which postulated that the nation would be officially neutral but would be prepared if events drew it into the war. Because of the small size of the U.S. military, many American officials argued that the nation's citizens should undertake military training to ensure the country was ready should war come. Concurrently, the United States took steps to professionalize its militia forces. By the early twentieth century, it was clear that the country's National Guard needed better training and equipment to support the Regular Army in the event of a mobilization.[4]

Scholars have long debated why the United States ended its neutrality and intervened in the war on the side of the Allies (Great Britain, France, Russia, and, later in the war, Italy). Some historians argue that the decision to intervene was based on the shared cultural heritage that naturally drew the United States into the conflict on the side of the Allies rather than Germany and the Central Powers (which also included Austria-Hungary and the Ottoman Empire). Surprisingly, perhaps, the theory of a shared loyalty and commonality between Great Britain and the United States has long been one of the weaker arguments to explain the American intervention. Such a theory fails to account for the large number of prominent American families with German ancestry. And while many politicians recognized the value of the country's relationship with Great Britain, President Wilson was not particularly interested in such strategic arguments as a cause for intervention.[5]

Another theory advanced to account for U.S. intervention focused on economics. The central argument of this theory depended on Great Britain's control of the seas. Without a doubt, as a major provider of food and war materiel to the Allies, American industry benefited from easier access to British and Allied ports. Furthermore, the need for supplies and materiel caused the Allies to borrow extensively from U.S. banking firms. Therefore, the argument runs, the United States intervened in 1917 to save the Allies from economic collapse. Indeed, even Wilson's secretary of state, William Jennings Bryan, wrote that "eastern financiers were forcing the nation into war in order to protect their war loans to the Allies."[6] It is true that by the time the U.S. entered the war in 1917, American bankers had already loaned more than $2 billion to the Allies. But historians Richard Hamilton and Holger Hellwig argue that such an economic interpretation of U.S. entry into the war "evaporates under scrutiny," primarily because the British went to great lengths to hide their financial troubles from the Americans and because blockades and other economic measures used by European powers during the war did not have the effect on the United States that they might have had a century earlier. Historian Justus Doenecke writes, "Wilson himself did not think in economic terms. Preserving Wall Street's stake in the Allied effort was far from his mind." While those theories offered clues to the U.S. intervention, they are not satisfactory explanations.[7] Hamilton and Hellwig cogently summed up the situation of the United States in 1917:

> Here was a big, geographically removed nation with a largely self-sufficient economy and a polyglot population, many of whose most recently arrived members had ties and feelings on opposing sides in the war. A tradition of diplomatic isolation and a century of nearly unbroken noninvolvement in overseas affairs had made foreign policy only a minor and intermittent concern in the nation's politics.[8]

So why did the United States intervene in 1917? Perhaps the best explanation has more to do with the decisions of the president than anything else. Under the leadership of President Wilson, the nation consciously moved from a policy of neutrality in 1914 to "armed neutrality" in 1915 and 1916 and then to war in 1917. As Wilson himself stated, "We are walking on quicksand."[9] Wilson's responses to several challenges from 1915 to 1917 brought the United States into the war on the side of the Allies.

President Woodrow Wilson is the central political figure in the American experience of World War I. From the time of his birth in 1856 in Virginia as the son of a Presbyterian preacher, Wilson learned lessons in morality and responsibility that he carried with him for the rest of his life. Elected president in 1912 after having served as the president of his alma mater, Princeton University, and as governor of New Jersey, Wilson identified with progressive sentiments and embraced reform. During his first term, he focused on business reform, with tariff, banking, and anti-trust legislation at the center of his work. By the election of 1916, however, he had begun a shift more toward social reform, such as women's suffrage and more stringent child labor laws. Until 1915, Wilson supported cuts in military appropriations and hoped the country could remain neutral in the war. His perspective began to change after the sinking of the *Lusitania* on May 7, 1915, by a German submarine, which claimed the lives of 128 Americans among the more than 1,000 civilians who perished. The deaths of the American passengers and the firm stance Wilson took in response to the sinking helped lead to the resignation of Secretary of State Bryan. From that point on, the president "single-handedly directed the nation's foreign affairs," and by July 1915 the shift from "preparedness" to "armed neutrality" had begun.[10]

Over the next year, Wilson engaged in what has been called a "diplomatic sparring match" with Germany over that nation's use of submarines. After the sinking of the *Sussex*, an English Channel ferry, in March 1916, Germany relented and pledged that its U-boats would no longer attack non-combatant ships of any kind. Wilson accepted the German pledge because he knew that no serious foreign policy initiatives could be taken until the result of the 1916 presidential election became known. Once he secured reelection in November 1916, and with rumblings that Germany was considering breaking the ban on unrestricted submarine warfare, Wilson began taking steps that he hoped would end the war in Europe; instead, they ultimately led to U.S. intervention. He asked the warring powers to publicly state their peace terms and promised that the United States would join a league of nations to help preserve future peace. In January 1917, he called for "peace without victory," in the hopes of achieving a non-punitive settlement to the war.[11]

Over the first few months of 1917, the president's commitment to "armed neutrality" gave way to intervention. This shift was not due solely to Wilson's changing attitudes but resulted from the German decision to resume unrestricted submarine warfare.[12] The resumption of unrestricted submarine warfare forced the president to respond. He did so by severing diplomatic relations with Germany in February 1917. Wilson next proposed legislation to arm American ships, a measure which passed in the U.S. House of Representatives, but failed in the Senate. In response to the action to stop the bill by what he termed a "little group of willful men," Wilson issued an executive order to arm the ships anyway. Despite this order, by March 21, six American ships had been sunk by Germany, and on April 2, 1917, Wilson asked Congress to declare war.[13] Wilson's speech making the case for war has been called one of the greatest ever given by an American president. Freshman Texas congressman Tom Connally listened to the speech, and although he claimed not to recall any of Wilson's specific points, he did remember that the president said "exactly what the Congress wanted to hear."[14] Wilson began by remarking on Germany's resumption of unrestricted submarine warfare, which he said meant that the government was setting aside "all restraints of law and of humanity" to sink every vessel that approached Great Britain and Ireland. Furthermore, the president observed, "I was for a little while unable to believe that such things would in fact be done by any government that had hitherto subscribed to the humane practices of civilized nations." But, to Wilson, such warfare was a "war against mankind" that had to be defeated. After stating his case, Wilson concluded his speech in a highly idealistic and persuasive manner:

It is a distressing and oppressive duty, Gentlemen of the Congress, which I have performed in thus addressing you. There are, it may be, many months of fiery trial and sacrifice ahead of us. It is a fearful thing to lead this great peaceful people into war, into the most terrible and disastrous of all wars, civilization itself seeming to be in the balance. But the right is more precious than peace, and we shall fight for the things which we have always carried nearest our hearts—for democracy, for the right of those who submit to authority to have a voice in their own Governments, for the rights and liberties of small nations, for a universal dominion of right by such a concert of free peoples as shall bring peace and safety to all nations and make the world itself at last free.[15]

After the speech, the Texas congressional delegation met for a discussion of Wilson's remarks. Connally recalled that they were all "deadly serious." As a member of the Foreign Affairs Committee, Connally attended an emergency committee meeting that voted on a war declaration. Connally later remembered that he felt a "cold chill" flow through his body as he voted in favor of war. After two days of debate in the Senate and four in the House, Congress passed the war declaration by a large majority: 82 to 6 in the Senate on

April 4, and 373 to 50 in the House on April 6, 1917. The nation was now at war, nearly three years after the fighting had begun in Europe.[16]

Earlier in 1917, as the United States teetered on the edge of war, Texas's geographical location brought the war closer to the state than most would have expected. The border region had become unsettled during the early twentieth century primarily because of the Mexican Revolution (1910–1920). In addition to the violence in Mexico associated with the revolution, other events in the years prior to the war served to increase tensions and violence along the border.[17]

Because of the Mexican Revolution, Texas received an influx of immigrants into South Texas, most of whom sought a secure future for themselves and their families. Many of these immigrants found employment in the local agricultural sector, but harsh working conditions strained relations with white landowners, many of whom were recent arrivals themselves from the American Midwest. In 1915, tensions boiled over with the discovery of a plot known as the Plan de San Diego. Allegedly written in the small South Texas town of San Diego in January 1915, the plan called for Mexican Americans, African Americans, and Japanese Americans to kill all white men over the age of sixteen. Although the plan scarcely existed as more than an idea, its discovery exacerbated tensions and spurred increased violence along the border. Texas Rangers, along with some vigilante groups, carried out extreme acts of violence against Mexicans. Even the adjutant general of Texas, Brigadier General Henry Hutchings, patrolled the border with a group of Texas Rangers. Hutchings would later play an important role in recruiting Texas National Guardsmen for service in World War I.[18]

A little over a year after the discovery of the Plan de San Diego, the U.S. government recognized Venustiano Carranza as the legitimate leader of Mexico, which touched off another round of violence along the border. Angered by the U.S. government's support of Carranza, one of his rivals, Francisco "Pancho" Villa, decided to seek revenge. He did this first by killing a group of American mining engineers who were traveling by train in Mexico and followed that attack with an even more audacious raid on Columbus, New Mexico, in March 1916. In response to this attack on American citizens within U.S. territory, President Wilson ordered Brigadier General John J. Pershing and approximately 10,000 soldiers into Mexico to capture Villa. Although they were not successful in capturing their quarry, the "Punitive Expedition" soon included the National Guard. The mobilization initially included only the National Guard of Texas, New Mexico, and Arizona. Soon, however, the president mobilized the entire U.S. National Guard, and by the summer of 1916 thousands of National Guardsmen arrived in South and West Texas to help secure the border. Although the National Guard never engaged in any major fighting with Mexican troops, the mobilization created an air of tension in Texas and other border states that was felt through the remainder of the year. Thus, fully a year before the United States entered the war, many Texans were already living with soldiers in their midst.[19]

Less than a year after Villa's raid and Pershing's Punitive Expedition, the Wilson administration publicly released the infamous Zimmermann Telegram on March 1, 1917. The British intercepted a telegram from the German foreign minister to the German ambassador to Mexico, which urged him to convince Mexico to support the Triple Alliance. In return for their support, Germany would help Mexico regain the territory it had lost to the United States in the U.S.–Mexico War of 1846–48. The British government forwarded the telegram to Washington, and President Wilson soon ordered it released to the public. While there was a strong outcry over the telegram, most of it focused on Germany rather than Mexico. The *Dallas Morning News* ran a front-page illustration that characterized the plot. Called "The Temptation," the illustration showed a large dark figure with horns, a spiked German helmet, and a thick mustache offering a sack of gold to a Mexican man wrapped in a blanket and sombrero (see illustration on p. 59). With his other hand, the large German figure pointed to a distant Texas, New Mexico, and Arizona. The cartoon implied that Germany sought to take advantage of Mexico, which many Texans certainly feared was possible at the time. For example, an editorial in the *Denton Record-Chronicle* lamented that "poor, feeble, strife-broken Mexico whose only chance for salvation lies in the friendship and support of the United States." After the telegram's release, the Mexican government denied being involved in such a plot. And while there was sympathy for the Mexican government, many Texans harbored no doubt of the outcome if Mexico supported Germany and an

9

invasion of Texas resulted. For example, the editor for the *Abilene Reporter* wrote that if a war with Mexico did break out "instead of Mexico getting Texas, New Mexico and Arizona it will wind up with Mexico annexed to the United States if there is any annexing." However, while most Texans blamed the Germans, a few were willing to point the finger closer to home. In Wichita Falls, the *Daily Times* believed that the release of the Zimmerman Telegram should "stir the patriotism even of some Texas representatives in Congress, whose attitude has been more likely to make them solid with those of alien sympathies."[20]

Although the Zimmermann Telegram remains a remarkable aspect of the war's prelude, a judicious examination of the topic by historian Thomas Boghardt reveals that the telegram did not significantly alter the opinion of many Americans toward intervention. Rather, the telegram appeared to have the most effect in areas where strong support for intervention already existed. Likewise, in areas where such sentiments were cooler, the telegram failed to sway public opinion in favor of intervention. It could be said that the Zimmermann Telegram added fuel to the fire rather than serving as a catalyst to change public opinion in support of intervention.[21]

Even if the Zimmermann Telegram did not have much effect on relations between the United States and Mexico, tensions along the border remained strained for most of the war. Newspaper articles routinely described numerous "German activities" taking place along the border, or alleged that Germans advised President Carranza, managed Mexican ammunition factories, and had even masterminded Pancho Villa's raid on Columbus. Sporadic incidents of violence along the border also continued throughout the war. For example, in July 1917, near the small town of Ojo de Agua in South Texas, a U.S. border patrol exchanged an estimated five hundred shots with an unknown number of Mexicans. In November, fighting between Pancho Villa's troops and Mexican government forces led to the capture of Ojinaga, a small town across the border from Presidio, Texas. After Villa's forces captured the town, the Mexican federal troops crossed the border and surrendered their weapons to U.S. soldiers. In some cases, U.S. troops fought Mexican government troops, while in others they battled cattle thieves who operated along the border. American troops also tracked down groups and individuals accused of robbery and murder. A particularly severe skirmish with Mexican bandits in the Big Bend area occurred on Christmas Day 1917. As was the case throughout the war, rampant rumors circulated that Mexican bandit raids into the Big Bend district had been "inspired" by Germans in cooperation with U.S. draft evaders south of the border. While U.S. Army Colonel George T. Langhorne, who commanded a cavalry regiment along the border, discounted such rumors, federal officials did investigate. As late as April 1918, U.S. authorities cut off the ability to make telephone calls between some Mexican and U.S. towns along the border because of the discovery of an "elaborate system of wire communication used by these plotting agents." In the months to come, the specter of German influence and money remained a factor in border tensions.[22]

Eventually, the U.S. Army formally activated the Fifteenth Cavalry Division of more than 18,000 troops. Headquartered at El Paso, this division was touted by the army as the largest body of cavalry under a single commander since the Civil War. Under the command of Major General George W. Read, the division consisted of three brigades, which were based in El Paso, San Antonio, and Douglas, Arizona. As a *New York Times* article about the division observed, "Any threatening developments in Mexico will find United States Cavalry firmly holding the north line of this country ready to put down lawlessness . . . there is sufficient infantry along the border to keep the peace, but infantry is most needed in the great struggle overseas. Cavalry, therefore, and especially this greatest body assembled in fifty years, will no doubt have the irksome job of riding the line for some time to come."[23] By the time American troops arrived in Europe, the United States border with Mexico was already militarized.

Woodrow Wilson's decision to intervene in the Great War raging in Europe had not come lightly. American political leaders operated within a national political tradition that reflected a general aversion to political involvement outside the Western Hemisphere. Such sentiments were long cemented within American political culture, and they remained a potent force in politics during the first decades of the twentieth century. Likewise, the Progressive movement also shaped politics during this period. The Progressive reform impulse was felt across the nation, and as historian Arthur Link observed, Progressivism emphasized economic and social justice. Applied to the country's foreign policy, that foundation found expression in support for the self-determination for the warring parties and "peace without victory" for all involved. Whether or not Wilson and the United States could bring that about, however, remained to be seen. The United States entered the conflict unprepared to fight a major war in Europe.[24]

*Chapter 2*

# TEXAS ENTERS THE GREAT WAR

In order to understand fully how World War I shaped Texas and affected the lives of its citizens, a survey of its political and economic conditions in 1914 is necessary. At the outset of the twentieth century, most Texans felt a connection to the state's nineteenth-century past. The legacies of the Texas Revolution and the Civil War remained strong in the minds of many, and the way those conflicts were remembered helped instill a belief in the superiority of Texas military prowess. While Texans entered the twentieth century with a conception of themselves as superior soldiers, they also thought of themselves as somewhat outside the American mainstream. They remembered the state's periods as an independent country and as part of the Confederacy.[1] By the time the First World War broke out, however, that conception was beginning to change.

According to the United States Census, Texas's population increased by nearly 1 million residents between 1910 and 1920, rising from 3.8 to 4.6 million. This growth helped initiate the state's transition from a rural and agricultural economy to a urbanizing, industrial one that would flourish in the later decades of the twentieth century. This industrialization was hastened even further by the discovery of Texas's massive oil fields, beginning with Spindletop in 1901.[2]

White residents remained a majority in the state, and the two largest minority groups were African Americans and Hispanics. Although the African American population increased to 741,000 by 1920, the proportion of black Texans declined relative to the state's total population. On the other hand, the Hispanic population grew very rapidly during the first two decades of the century, from an estimated 71,000 in 1900 to approximately 251,000 by

1920, many of whom had migrated north from Mexico in order to escape the violence associated with the Mexican Revolution.[3]

While those minority populations increased in the years before World War I, a culture of segregation marginalized blacks and Hispanics as second-class citizens. In common with other southern states, Texas enacted a range of "Jim Crow" segregation laws, which gave the state's black population little chance either of participating in local or state government or of improving themselves socially and economically. The Jim Crow laws were also applied to black soldiers who were stationed in Texas, and several times in the early years of the century black soldiers retaliated when they failed to receive the respect, dignity, and equality they were entitled to as U.S. soldiers. Instances of racial violence involving black soldiers took place in several Texas cities, including Brownsville, Laredo, Del Rio, and El Paso. Incidents of an even more violent character would rock both Houston and Waco in the summer of 1917. (Both of those incidents received national attention and will be discussed in greater detail in chapter 3.) The lynching of black Texans was not uncommon in the early twentieth century. In fact, eighty black Texans lost their lives through lynching and mob violence in the new century's first decade. While Hispanics were not subject to the same Jim Crow laws as blacks, they faced similar forms of discrimination. As an example, voting laws that implemented poll taxes and ballots printed only in English provided ways to disfranchise both blacks and Hispanics. Despite these affronts, African Americans and Hispanics contributed greatly to the war effort. In fact, more than 31,000 black Texans served with the armed forces during World War I.[4]

Texas was also home to nearly 240,000 foreign-born residents, and an additional 350,000 had foreign-born parents. Of the foreign-born residents, the 1910 census counted approximately 45,000 Germans and 20,000 Austrians in Texas. Thus, nearly 65,000 Texans had been born in nations that fought against the Allies. However, the fear of foreigners would far outweigh the actual numbers of foreign-born residents of the state, who represented just a fraction of the total population of Texas.[5]

The majority of Texans in the 1910s still lived in rural areas, and agriculture was the most important part of the state's economy. Although ranching had long been a viable economic pursuit and

Texas led the nation in cattle production, cotton remained the state's "money crop." In 1910, Texas agriculture outpaced all other states except Iowa and Illinois in total crop value, and by 1920 Texas exceeded all other states in the total value of agricultural production. Two-thirds of Texans lived in municipalities with populations less than 2,500. Nevertheless, urbanization had begun, and by 1920 four Texas cities had populations greater than 100,000. San Antonio was the largest, and Dallas, Houston, and Fort Worth followed. Eight other cities had populations of greater than 20,000 by 1920. And although Texas lagged behind industrial stalwarts such as New York, Pennsylvania, and Ohio, industry and manufacturing were on the upswing thanks to the nascent but booming oil industry. In 1915, Texas produced 24 million barrels of oil, and with the discovery of several new oilfields, the state reached 38 million barrels in 1918. In 1919 Texas produced 79 million barrels, more than tripling its 1915 production.[6]

From a political perspective, single-party politics dominated the state's political culture. The Democratic Party wielded vast political power in Texas, while the Republican Party remained small and fractured. Reflecting the dominance of the Democratic Party in state politics, most Texans supported President Wilson in the elections of 1912 and 1916. When war broke out in Europe in 1914, Oscar Colquitt governed the state. During the American participation in the war James E. Ferguson and William P. Hobby led the state. Ferguson, a native of Bell County, was born in 1871. Campaigning as "Farmer Jim," Ferguson aimed to connect with the state's rural majority and won election in 1914. He proved to be such a popular governor that he won a second term in 1916. After that, however, his fortunes sank once he became embroiled in a fight against the University of Texas that focused on the school's budget and several faculty members that he wanted to see removed from their posts. This fracas with the university resulted in the state legislature investigating Ferguson's finances and led to an attempt to impeach the governor, which forced him from office in September 1917. Although Ferguson served as governor during the initial months of the American intervention and helped expand the Texas National Guard, his struggles with the University of Texas quickly drew his focus away from the war effort. His resignation, however, opened the door for Lieutenant Governor William P. Hobby to assume leadership of the state. Hobby had worked his way up through the newspaper business and had been managing editor of the *Houston Post* prior to his election as lieutenant governor in 1914.[7]

Although dominated by a single party, fierce political conflict still occurred as conservative Democrats vied with Progressives, who sought various types of reform, whether political, social, or economic. In the main, however, Texas Democrats in the early twentieth century favored limited taxes, controlled spending, and showed little appetite for programs to help blacks, Hispanics, and poor whites. Nevertheless, the Progressive reform impulse championed two issues that were resolved during and immediately after the war: Prohibition and woman's suffrage. The war shaped debate on both issues, and politicians sought to link their support of those causes to the war effort.

Opposing groups of Texas voters and politicians, breaking along lines of ethnicity and religious affiliation, had wrangled over Prohibition for decades on the eve of the Great War: German Texans and Catholics generally opposed Prohibition, whereas Anglo Protestants were Prohibition's most vocal supporters. But Prohibition gained renewed support because of efforts to ban alcohol from areas around military training sites. In fact, the Texas legislature passed four laws aimed at protecting soldiers from the "evil influence of intoxicating liquors," one of which stipulated a ten-mile "dry" zone around military camps, while a second prevented "immoral practices," or prostitution, in the hopes of protecting soldiers from the "diseases which follow in the wake of vice." Thus, Prohibition's supporters successfully linked their efforts at banning alcohol with the health and welfare of American soldiers.[8]

The Prohibition movement had been an important vehicle for women's involvement in politics, and as proponents of Prohibition made gains during the war years, so did those who advocated more political rights for women. Texans who supported giving full voting rights for women also cast their efforts in light of the war effort. Led by such activists as Minnie Fisher Cunningham, the Texas Equal Suffrage Association attempted to highlight the patriotic service of Texas women involved in wartime activities such as the Red Cross and Liberty Bond drives. Suffragists also argued that Americans were fighting to "save democracy" overseas while limiting the rights of some of its citizens at home. Those efforts spurred the women's suffrage movement during the war, and although Texas governor William P. Hobby supported legislation to allow women to vote in Texas primaries, full suffrage for women in Texas failed until the summer of 1919 when Congress submitted a constitutional amendment to allow women to vote. Texas served as a bellwether for other states, and President Wilson sent a cable to Minnie Fisher Cunningham that read, in part, "I am looking forward with the greatest interest to the referendum of May 24 on woman suffrage, and entertain the confident hope that the men of Texas will by a very great majority render gallant justice to the women of the state." Texas became the ninth state to ratify the amendment after Governor Hobby called the legislature into special session. Women had been allowed to vote in the 1918 primaries, and they accounted for more than 320,000 of the 700,000 votes cast. Women voters also turned out to support incumbent Governor Hobby, which enabled him to defeat former Governor James Ferguson as well as six members of the Texas congressional delegation who had tried to unseat Hobby in 1918.[9]

Texas politicians at the federal level also shaped the state's response to the Great War—sometimes in ways that put them at odds with their constituents. Both Texas senators wielded considerable political power. Charles A. Culberson was the state's senior senator, having been elected as the Texas attorney general in 1890 and as governor in 1894. In 1899, he moved to the Senate and began a twenty-four-year career in the upper house. Sixty-two years old at the start of the war, Culberson was in poor health due in part to a struggle with alcoholism; nevertheless, he was a strong supporter of the Wilson administration and used his position as the chairman of the Senate Judiciary Committee to support the president. Culberson introduced several pieces of legislation both prior to and after the declaration of war, one of which sought to punish "acts of interference with the foreign relations, the neutrality, and the foreign commerce of the United States," and the second to "punish the destruction or injuring of war material and war transportation facilities by fire, explosives, or other violent means." Those would later become the Espionage Act of 1917 and the Sedition Act of 1918. Culberson also added his name to a joint resolution that authorized the president to seize any vessel belonging to a country at war with the United States. Culberson's junior colleague was forty-two-year old Morris Sheppard. A native Texan born in 1875, Sheppard attended the University of Texas and Yale and in 1902 won election to the U. S. House of Representatives to a seat once held by his father. In 1913, Texans elected him to the Senate, where he also proved to be a supporter of the Wilson administration. Sheppard was responsible for several key pieces of legislation during the war, including a bill to create an aviation division within the War Department. More importantly, his support for Prohibition would lead him to introduce legislation into the Senate that eventually became the nation's Eighteenth Amendment. A master at equating the welfare of America's soldiers with Prohibition, Sheppard declared that the warring powers were aware that "the liquor habit is their deadliest enemy." Describing how most of the major powers restricted their troops' use of alcohol, Sheppard agreed with Kaiser Wilhelm II of Germany, who had allegedly stated that "the dominant nation of the future would be the nation consuming the least amount of alcohol." Thus, from Sheppard's perspective, stopping the sale of liquor to the "civic soldiers, the economic soldiers, at home" was as important as fighting on the battlefield, and he looked forward to the day when the United States would "see a saloon-less nation and a spotless flag." While the voting for what would become the Eighteenth Amendment did not take place until 1919, Sheppard's fellow Senator Charles Culberson voted against Prohibition. Prohibition became the law of the land until repealed in 1933. Sheppard remained a powerful senator for several decades after the war. He retired in 1941.[10]

The Texas delegation to the House of Representatives offered several responses to the war, most in a support of the Wilson administration, but one Texas congressman remained a vocal opponent. The delegation consisted of eighteen members, sixteen from the state's congressional districts and two "at-large" seats. They were all men and all Democrats, and the majority supported the war declaration. Of the four who were critical of President Wilson's policies, only one, Atkins "Jeff" McLemore, would go so far as to vote against the declaration of war. Texas representatives participated in the debates on the war declaration and conscription, introduced wartime legislation or facilitated its passage, served on congressional committees, and worked to get military bases in their state. Included among the several bills they introduced was Daniel

Garrett's bill to provide $10 million for soldiers' wives, children, and dependent mothers. Marvin Jones introduced legislation that suspended the statute of limitations for "all crimes and offenses against the United States during the war with Germany," and James L. Slayden introduced a bill to tax high explosives to earn revenue. Future vice president John Nance Garner served as the liaison between President Wilson and the House of Representatives, while other members of the delegation traveled to Europe in 1918 as part of an official delegation, where they had the chance to fly over the Western Front in a "battleplane." One member, Tom Connally, joined the U.S. Army toward the end of the war.[11]

While Senators Culberson and Sheppard were not particularly vocal during the war declaration debate in April 1917, Sheppard signaled his sympathies by entering several letters and telegrams from "sundry citizens of Texas, expressing practically unanimous support of the President," into the *Congressional Record*. Such telegrams expressed the general sentiment across the state in favor of the war declaration. For example, a letter from Cooke County, along the Red River, read, "True American citizens and Texans look to our able senators to stand in our behalf for absolute loyalty to our great President and the administration." Likewise, the mayor of Terrell in Dallas County wrote that "the people of this section of Texas are squarely behind the President in his stand to protect American rights, and I am sure that all true and loyal Texans desire that you support the President." In general, the letters indicate sympathy with President Wilson's policies; many of the telegrams claimed they expressed the "unanimous sentiment of the people . . . of the state." Of course, such sentiments were not unique to Texas.[12]

On the other hand, the Texas delegation to the House of Representatives was much more vocal in expressing their opinions during the debates on the war declaration. Representative James L. Slayden used biblical language when he spoke to the House on April 5: "I have hoped against hope that this cup might pass. But it must be drained, bitter as it is." While he considered the war vote the most important since the Civil War, he also believed that it would force the country to abandon the Monroe Doctrine of non-interference in conflict outside the Western Hemisphere. Although he stated that he had "spent anxious days and sleepless nights trying in vain to devise some means by which my country might be spared this trial," his efforts to bring the war to a conclusion without American intervention had failed. Slayden concluded his remarks by stating, "I am an American, and, greatly as I deplore the situation, I shall, much as it distresses me, stand by my country."[13]

Representative Joe Eagle of Houston left no doubt about his stance and opened his remarks by stating clearly, "Mr. Chairman, without any mental reservation whatsoever, I give my voice and my vote to this resolution. It states the truth in plain, simple words." Eagle then reviewed the circumstances that led to the war declaration, calling Kaiser Wilhelm II a "cave man" and thundering that Germany had "uniformly perverted the truth, broken the faith of their treaties, persistently violated the law of nations, trampled underfoot the highest rights of humanity, filled the world with conscienceless spies." The House applauded Eagle throughout this speech.[14]

Again, the lone dissenting voice belonged to Atkins "Jeff" McLemore.[15] McLemore, a Tennessee native who lived in Austin, favored isolationism and sent mixed messages to his constituents in his "at large" district, and he would later lose his seat for his lack of support for the war effort. In fact, his stance spurred the *Houston Post* to quip, "We haven't sifted out the partisan aspects of it, but quite a number of congressmen have already commenced their campaign for retirement next year with every prospect of success." When he spoke in Congress, McLemore stated that "as much as I may wish to stand by the President in all things, yet I cannot, by any force of reasoning, bring myself to believe that a vote for this resolution will be right and just or that in casting such vote I will be voicing the sentiment of a majority of the people I have the honor to represent." McLemore offered several reasons for not supporting the war declaration. First, like Slayden, he expressed concern over foreign alliances. Second, he believed the taxes necessary to pay for the war would become "a millstone around the necks of the American people" for years. And finally, he believed that a war declaration would give President Wilson "absolute" power. McLemore stressed that he was not a pacifist and had supported the Preparedness Movement. Furthermore, he understood the personal risk he took in opposing the war and that he would likely draw a "storm of abuse and censure" from his constituents. He could tolerate that, he

said, because he had the "inner consciousness of doing that which
I believe to be right."[16]
As he expected, McLemore received significant criticism for his
dissenting vote. The following telegram from "district, state, and
county officers" of Wharton is worth quoting in full as it exempli-
fies the criticism he received:

We notice from the press dispatch today that you stated you
could not support the war resolution and further stated that your
action represented the sentiment of the majority of your constituents in Texas. We feel, as American citizens and as citizens of
Texas, we would be remiss in our duty to our state and country
to allow such statement made by a person holding the position
you hold to go unchallenged, and we here now say to you that
your action does not represent the sentiments of your constituents
or an appreciable percentage. We say to you that we believe you
know that the sentiments of the citizens of Texas are practically
unanimously in favor of the resolution, and we are at a loss to
account for your actions.[17]

McLemore had also opposed other war-related measures and
had introduced legislation in Congress that would require American citizens travelling on armed merchant ships be made aware of
the danger they faced from surprise submarine attacks. Known as
the Gore-McLemore Resolutions, they were described by oppo-
nents as a "resolution of cowardice and surrender", and were
soundly defeated after President Wilson expressed his opposition.
Five of his fellow Texas congressmen voted against McLemore's
resolution. McLemore was up for election in 1918 because his
"at large" seat had been eliminated. Without a doubt, his opposition to the war declaration negatively influenced his prospects
for reelection. In fact, after the 1918 elections, the *New York
Times* reported that McLemore was beaten in every county in his
district. As the paper stated, "He was third, and a limping third at
that." While McLemore bore the brunt of criticism for his actions,
other members of the Texas delegation were not immune from
political barbs.[18]
In addition to the state's senators and representatives, several
other Texans, either as members of President Wilson's cabinet or as

unofficial advisors, played important roles in developing and implementing U.S. policy during the war. The most well-known unofficial advisor to the president during the war was "Colonel" Edward M. House. A native Texan, House came from a wealthy family and had advised several Texas governors. He had even been made an honorary colonel in the Texas militia in 1892 after helping Governor James Hogg win reelection. During the election of 1912, House became close to Wilson and probably would have been offered any cabinet position he desired in the new administration. He declined to accept one, however, and instead chose to serve in an unofficial capacity, where he came to wield considerable influence with the president. Known as the "Texas Sphinx," House was described by historian Justus Doenecke as a combination of Wilson's "chief of staff, national security advisor, and chief diplomatic agent." Even so, House's influence began to wane as early as the spring of 1915, when the president began to turn to his second wife, Edith Bolling Galt, for counsel. Nevertheless, House did play an important role in the events leading up to U.S. intervention in the war and led a major diplomatic mission to Europe in October 1917. His contributions and relationship with Wilson have been the subject of continued study since the end of the war.[19]

Other Texans who served the Wilson administration more formally, and often controversially, included Postmaster General Albert Sidney Burleson, Attorney General Thomas Watt Gregory, and Agriculture Secretary David F. Houston. In March 1917, Houston, along with the other Texans in the president's cabinet, urged President Wilson to intervene in the war. Referring to Germany, he said, "We see what she is trying to do against us in Mexico. We ought to recognize that a state of war exists." Another well-known Texan who contributed to the war effort at the national level was fifty-seven-year old Robert S. Lovett of San Jacinto. In the summer of 1917, Lovett, chairman of the executive committee of the Union Pacific Railroad, was selected as one of the seven members of the War Industries Board. The War Industries Board oversaw the government's expenditures related to the war effort and dealt with questions of cost and prioritization. When Lovett later left the War Industries Board, his replacement was Edwin B. Parker of Houston. Dallas's Thomas B. Love was also appointed as an assistant secretary of the Treasury Department in 1917.[20]

The Texas state government also supported the war declaration, although the Texas House did not formally issue a resolution calling for Texas to endorse the actions of the federal government until August 1917. In part, the resolution stated that President Wilson should be "reassured of the sympathy, loyalty and fidelity of the people of the state of Texas to the cause for which we fight." Furthermore, the Texas legislature implemented several laws to support Texas soldiers, including two that gave soldiers relief from creditors and the right to defer bills until ninety days after a peace treaty had been signed. Governor Hobby also called the legislature to its fourth session during the war to enact "certain laws for the purpose of protecting soldiers in training in Texas and to render the state of Texas more efficient as an agency for winning the war." And in a 1919 address to the state legislature, Hobby asserted that the purpose of such legislation had been to "protect the interest of the soldier who is fighting for us, and to relieve his mind of the worry and uneasiness which might greatly interfere with his work."[21]

The social, political, and economic context of the first two decades of the twentieth century shaped the way Texans understood their roles in the war effort. Attached to memories of Texas's time as an independent republic and still tied strongly to the southern states it had joined in the Confederacy, including a strong rural and agricultural orientation, Texans tended to think of themselves as something of a breed apart in a nation that was rapidly industrializing and urbanizing. However, economic, demographic, and technological changes brought Texans closer to the American mainstream by 1914. In this context Texans watched the war unfold in Europe, and Texas leaders at the state and national levels helped shape the decisions that affected the course of the nation's response to the war, and prepared to send its sons to fight in the trenches of the Western Front. One thing that remained constant was pride in the Texas tradition of battlefield success, and the state's residents would face the current conflict with confidence.

# Chapter 3

# THE HOME FRONT

On the day Congress declared war against Germany, more than two hundred "prominent men" of the Civilian Training Camp Association met at San Antonio's Gunter Hotel to hear Major General John J. Pershing speak on the Preparedness Movement and an upcoming training camp to be held in Austin in May 1917.[1] Joining Pershing at the head table were senior Regular Army officers from nearby Fort Sam Houston, Texas National Guard officers, and the mayor of San Antonio, Clinton G. Brown, who had previously attended a preparedness camp and wore his uniform to the meeting. At the time, Pershing commanded the Southern Department of the U.S. Army and hoped to recruit for the civilian training camp in Austin, which was the first of five scheduled to open in the summer of 1917. Pershing hoped that each camp would have at least five thousand men and stated that the United States could produce "an army equal to any in the world," if it was done in "a careful manner, wisely and systematically." The local San Antonio newspaper observed that the meeting "grew into a grand demonstration of patriotism and almost every speaker was cheered to the echo when mention was made of loyalty to the president and to the country at this critical time."[2]

As that meeting indicated, most Texans greeted the American intervention in the war enthusiastically. The headline of the *Houston Post*'s Saturday edition blared "WAR" and printed the war proclamation in full. Communities across the state reacted immediately to the declaration of war. Cities and towns held rallies, picnics, and parades to show their support for the Wilson administration. Newspapers served as the voice of local elites, who encouraged patriotic support of the war. In Denton, for example, the mayor posted a "Call to All Americans" in the local paper to draw support for a meeting in which attendees were urged to "endorse by your presence the course of our nation in this time of grave impact." The meeting drew nearly eight thousand people from the community. The headlines of other papers told the same story: "Flag Stock at Hearne Depleted," "San Angelo Gives Demonstration," "Belton Patriots Hold Rousing Meeting," "Patriotism Dominates Gonzales," and "Patriotism Strikes Tuleta." The city of Austin declared April 9, 1917, to be "Loyalty Day," and the mayor promised a half-day holiday and a parade of thousands. Indeed, at the urging of local officials, stores in cities and towns across the state closed their doors to allow their employees to show their support for the war. Business owners who believed making money was more important than participating in a parade had to tread carefully lest they were perceived as disloyal. Indeed, the *Abilene Reporter* reminded its readers that once war had been declared, loyalty demanded that all "criticism of the President and the Congress shall cease." The paper also went so far as to say that no citizen now had the right to "speak against his country no matter how much he detests war."[3]

The parades and rallies and support for the war effort highlighted the importance that many Texans placed on military service, either by the raising of volunteer companies or by creating "home guards," which were often led by veterans. Raising local soldiers within a single community had long been a key component of the volunteer tradition within the United States and had been used in the Texas Revolution and the Civil War. In the spring and summer months of 1917, Texas had its share of men who looked to raise their own companies, either for service on the Western Front or as home guards to protect local communities. In fact, many communities sought veterans who could provide rudimentary military instruction to locals. In Wise County, at the conclusion of a patriotic rally, a veteran took charge of a group of local men and marched them around the courthouse square while more than two hundred people watched the proceedings. In Abilene, there was talk of "military training for the business men," while in Houston, the *Post* announced that an "experienced drill master" would be at the intersection of Main and Lamar Streets to provide an hour's instruction every day to "all men, old or young, who attend." An editorial in the *Post* stressed the importance of military readiness associated with these drills: "The end of the war with Germany may be but the beginning of other conflicts. We may find an enemy closer to us than any European power. Invasion of our own land is not an impossibility. War upon the fields of Texas is not beyond the powers of the imagination. Home Guards may be needed."[4]

In fact, many communities considered the establishment of home guard companies as a way to show their communities' commitment to the war effort and as protection from the perceived threat from Mexico. For example, in Lockhart, locals organized a "Rifle Club" after the war declaration with the intention of serving as a home guard, and in Waco, the *Dallas Morning News* observed that the formation of a home guard company was a sign that "our citizens are alive to the real meaning of preparedness. We do not anticipate that Texas will feel the shock of the coming war with Germany . . . We trust that Teuton-Inspired revolution will not upset the Mexican government and then under the Kaiser's direction turn toward the Rio Grande." Other communities went so far as to inform the state's congressional leaders of their plans. One citizen of San Benito wired Senator Sheppard that he could raise a "full regiment of experienced and expert rifle shots," with no trouble.[5]

Too old to serve in 1917, veterans of both the Civil War and the Spanish-American War assumed a greater role in forming many home guard companies. For example, one company in Abilene included veterans in their sixties and seventies who displayed the "enthusiasm of younger men." In Amarillo, an aged group of Civil War veterans formed a home guard to "take care of any demonstration or disorder which might arise in the area" as a result of the release of the Zimmermann Telegram, although the level of protection that such home guard companies could provide to a community was minimal. Still, they did illustrate one of the ways that local communities supported the war effort.[6]

Indeed, Civil War veterans, Union and Confederate, were held in high esteem in World War I-era Texas and were frequently the guests of honor at rallies and marched in parades in communities across the state. However, the strong dedication to loyalty and patriotism was such that even Civil War veterans were not immune to suspicion. In one case in 1918, an old Confederate veteran reportedly failed to keep his hat removed as the U.S. flag was carried by in a parade. Placing his hat back on his head before the flag had completely passed by angered onlookers so much that he was taken to the federal building and warned to be careful in the future.[7] Raising such local companies of militia or home guards was not unique to Texas. Former president Theodore Roosevelt employed the same concept when he attempted to recruit soldiers for service on the Western Front, as he had done with the famed Rough Riders in the Spanish-American War. In 1917, Roosevelt attempted to raise a volunteer division he would personally lead into battle, just as he had done nearly two decades earlier. In 1898, Roosevelt recruited many of his Rough Riders at San Antonio's Menger Hotel, and after the United States entered World War I he dispatched recruiters to Texas to raise a squadron of cavalry for his division. One of Roosevelt's recruiters was quoted as saying, "We are receiving many applications from good men all over Southwest Texas who are simply rearing to get into the game." The recruiter added, "A good troop is being organized at Del Rio, which will include men from Sonora, San Angelo and Rock Springs, where some real, live ranger riders are to be found." The Texas Legislature even extended an invitation to Roosevelt to speak in May 1917. While it seems many Texans were eager to join Roosevelt's volunteer division, President Wilson had no enthusiasm for allowing a potential rival like Roosevelt to lead a division overseas, particularly one that he had recruited. Thus, Roosevelt's "division" would not see service in Europe, and Roosevelt himself would die shortly after the end of the war. Although the administration declined to use locally raised amateur troops for service in the war, the spirit of volunteerism remained strong.[8]

In a speech in San Antonio on the day war was declared, General Pershing stressed that "every organization and every citizen can do a part." Likewise, a *Houston Post* editorial thundered, "Every man and woman who has time not needed for themselves must dedicate it to the country." At both the state and national level, several different organizations were established that allowed individuals to participate in the war. The best-known of those wartime organization was the American Red Cross, although it had not been created in response to World War I. During the first few months after the war declaration, Red Cross chapters sprang up in cities and towns across the state. As one Amarillo editor gushed, "Every thriving city in the panhandle of Texas should begin the organization of a Red

Cross Society" in order to be considered "progressive and patriotic." Women also participated significantly in Red Cross chapters across the state, regardless of their social status. For example, Willie May Kell, the daughter of a prominent Wichita Falls resident, spoke during the first draft registration on June 5, 1917. During her speech, she took her fellow women to task for not showing enough interest in the organization. The Red Cross also recruited female doctors, including Ellen C. Cover of San Antonio and Mary Agnes Hopkins of Dallas, to serve in France. And those who did not have the time to devote to the Red Cross could still participate by donating items. As one newspaper article stated, "You may have often wished that you could help the suffering soldiers in their trenches, the helpless wounded on the gory battlefields of France, or the moaning, battered men on hospital cots in the war zone. This is your chance." Texans also participated in the Red Cross at the national level, such as Rice Institute professor Stockton Axson, who served as the society's national secretary, and Houston businessman Jesse H. Jones, who served as the Director General of Military Relief of the American Red Cross.[9]

The Council of National Defense also offered opportunities for Texans to serve in varying capacities. Like the Red Cross, the Council of National Defense spearheaded efforts to recruit medical personnel to assist in the United States and overseas. In 1918, the National Council of Defense called on the states to furnish as many as 12,000 doctors to support the U.S. Army and Navy, with each state receiving a quota. The council asked the Lone Star State to provide 150 doctors to support that effort. Likewise, each state established a state Council of Defense that served to connect the national government to the state level, while the state council, in turn, served as a bridge to the county level. Modeled after the National Council of Defense, Governor Ferguson signed the bill authorizing a state council in May 1917 with an appropriation of $35,000. In order to confer legitimacy and authority, Governor Ferguson's legislation delegated to the state council the same powers that Congress had given to the National Council. In general, State Councils of Defense carried out several functions, including coordinating agricultural and industrial programs, developing propaganda materials, supporting Liberty Loan drives, helping with selective service (draft) registration, and even assisting law enforcement authorities in their search for "slackers." As one local newspaper observed, the councils were there to "promote the patriotic spirit of the people, aid in recruiting the state and National Guard and the regular army, [and] to aid in getting idle boys and men to work on the farm." To do this, the state councils established county-level counterparts. During the war, Texas established 240 county Councils of Defense and more than 15,000 community-level councils. The majority of county-level councils had begun their work in earnest by the time the first draftees had departed for training by September 1917.[10]

The state and local councils of defense consisted of prominent members of the community. While men held the positions on the state's executive council, women served at the county level in places like Wichita Falls, Cleburne, and Gainesville. The county-level councils mirrored the state-level organization and consisted of sub-committees to handle various issues such as publicity, finance, sanitation and medicine, food supply and conservation, labor, and the military. Local councils served as community focal points for all things related to the war.[11]

While the Red Cross and the councils of defense were large organizations that spread throughout the state in response to new conditions, Texas's agricultural sector, already strong, was one of state's most prominent means of supporting the war. One day after the war declaration, the *Houston Post* printed the following statement that highlighted the important role of Texas agriculture: "Don't sell the old hen if she is laying, unless you are bound to have the money. Let her lay for the country while the country is laying for the Kaiser." Indeed, the *Houston Post* continued to stress the importance of agriculture in the war effort: "Let every farmer remember that the plow at work is equal to a machine gun and a hoe in action is as good as a rifle." Likewise, the *Post* stated that "the United States expects every cotton farmer to feed himself and help feed the others. The food raiser will get his reward in money and in the satisfaction which comes of knowing he has truly served his country." Because Texas had an abundance of wheat, farmers across the state offered their excess grain crop to feed European refugees. As one newspaper editor wrote in May 1917, "The hungry world will surely hear with satisfaction that the Texans have started their reapers to going, and that the crop, if not as good as it might be, is also a lot better than it might be." Although faced with a severe drought,

Texas farmers produced enough to allow the residents of Grimes County, located between Houston and College Station, to offer its entire 1918 wheat harvest to the war effort, selling it at cost to the government. In response, Food Administrator and future President Herbert Hoover wired his thanks to local officials. The Grimes County sale was just a fraction of at least 80,000,000 bushels of wheat that the United States sent to Europe between July 1917 and March 1918. Texans donated more than wheat. During the war, Texans donated beef, pork, and sugar, among other foodstuffs. In addition, as harvest time approached in 1918, hundreds of women volunteered to work on local farms. Known as the Women's Land Army, hundreds of Texas women helped to bring in crops across the state. This effort piqued the interest of the *New York Times*, which reported that while some farmers had been "slow to accept women for farm labor," they were always "glad to take them a second time." Residents of Texas cities and towns were even encouraged to plant gardens in unused city lots. In Amarillo, for example, approximately 80 acres of vacant lot space were used to produce an estimated 40,000 pounds of beans and peas.[12]

Besides farming and ranching, Texans contributed to the war through the large shipbuilding industry in Houston, Beaumont, Orange, and Rockport. Once the United States declared war on Germany, the U.S. government sought to increase its fleet of merchant vessels. By the summer of 1917, the government, through the Emergency Fleet Corporation under the authority of Major General George Goethals, had contracted for 104 ships: 38 of steel, 34 made entirely of wood, 32 that used both, and several that were all concrete. These ships were scheduled for delivery in 1918. The government also contracted for the building of 72 wooden hulls. Nine Texas shipbuilding companies, in turn, secured contracts to build some of those ships, primarily the wooden ones. Houston-based Universal Shipbuilding Company built twelve of the wooden hulls while four more were built in Beaumont. In May 1918, the *City of Bonham*, 320 feet long and 47 feet wide, one of the largest wooden ships ever built, was launched. The U.S. Shipping Board considered the ship to be the model for the future. More of the contracted ships were launched on July 4, 1918, to patriotic celebrations. Ships launched on that day included the 4,700-ton *Beechland* and the 3,500-ton *Arenac* in Orange, the 3,500-ton *Quapaw* and

*Arado* from Beaumont, and the 3,500-ton *Banicaa* and *Katonah*, both built in Houston. In 1918, Texas shipbuilders completed more than 20 wooden ships, and by the time the war ended, Texans had built more than 120 wooden steamships to support the war.[13]

Texans also participated in the famous Liberty Loan campaigns. The Liberty Loan served as a means for the government to raise money, while subscribers purchased bonds to show their patriotism, loyalty, and support of the government. The First Liberty Loan campaign, held in May 1917, looked to raise two billion dollars, and Texans were expected to support it fully. As former Dallas mayor Henry D. Lindsey stated, "Texas was never in better financial condition in all of her history . . . And the people of Texas, from the highest to the lowest, are solidly behind the Administration in the war. We are going to have [a] splendid cotton crop and we are going to get big prices for it. So my prediction of the success of the Liberty Loan in Texas is based on those two solid reasons—we have the money and we are for the war."[14]

As predicted, the Liberty Loan campaign received more than enough support. For example, the Dallas Federal Reserve District reported subscriptions totaling more than $42 million, beating its allotment by more than $2 million. To meet its goals, the Dallas Federal Reserve enlisted telephone operators to call people in their district to leave the following message: "Federal Reserve Bank wants to know if you have bought your Liberty Bond. If not, they want you to see your banker today."[15]

Support for the Liberty Loan program did not end with the first campaign but continued through three more campaigns until the war ended. In the second and third campaigns, the majority of Texas cities reached or exceeded their quotas. For example, Galveston, Austin, Waco, and El Paso each drew between 25,000 and 50,000 subscribers for the third loan, while San Antonio, Houston, Fort Worth, and Dallas each managed between 50,000 and 100,000 Liberty Loan subscribers. While support was strong, fears of espionage and sabotage leaked into the campaigns. In October 1917, for example, the *New York Times* reported that pro-German "agents" had attempted to defeat the Liberty Loan program, and "their organized propaganda is alleged to have borne fruit in scattered localities from Minnesota to Texas, where weak efforts have been made, not openly, but by indirect methods, to discourage subscriptions." Many of those efforts entailed personal advice given to individuals not to participate, interfering with campaign publicity, and exerting pressure on banks who supported the Liberty Loan campaigns. While such efforts did not materially amount to much, they added to the air of suspicion and fear among many communities across Texas and the nation.[16]

Colleges and universities across Texas joined in the war effort, either on their own or in conjunction with the armed forces. First, in addition to its flying fields, the U.S. Army Air Service established ground training schools to train aviation cadets at six universities, including the University of Texas. The ground training school was held at Austin's Penn Field, which, in addition to the School of Military Aeronautics, also operated a radio school that trained radio operators from March 1918 until August 1919. The School of Military Aeronautics offered a twelve-week ground school that could accommodate more than 1,400 cadets. Once a cadet completed the ground training curriculum, which included physical fitness, military drill, courses in bombing, wireless and signaling, the theory of flight, types of aircraft, aircraft maintenance, map reading, photography, and many other subjects, they were sent to the Camp Dick aviation camp at the Texas State Fairgrounds in Dallas until receiving orders to report to one of the state's many airfields. The training was not easy, as one editorial confirmed: "There is no opportunity in military aviation for a man who is only half way good. But for the competent there is the opportunity to play an important part in ending the war."[17]

In addition to the University of Texas, the army worked with an assortment of schools around the state to establish U.S. Army training detachments and Students' Army Training Corps (SATC) units. By the time those units were fully functional in the fall of 1918, the armistice was only weeks away, although military leaders did not know how close the end of the war was at the time. Nevertheless, the number of schools that hosted SATC units was impressive and included public and private universities and colleges, from the largest to the smallest. At least thirty-one colleges and universities across the state participated. The Agricultural and Mechanical College of Texas (now known as Texas A&M University) also hosted a Reserve Officer Training Corps (ROTC) detachment, which had opened in October 1916. Unofficially, some schools, such as Houston's Rice Institute (now Rice University) offered credit to students who were satisfactorily enrolled in courses if they joined the military. Rice also developed its own military training course. As the *Houston Post* observed, "Preparations are now under way at the institute to give the students a military training course under a competent and regular army officer who has been secured." That evolved into its own ROTC detachment, which opened in October 1917. Of course, large numbers of recent graduates from Texas universities served in the military during the war. For example, in July 1918, the University of Texas boasted that more than 1,700 former students had joined the military, while Texas A&M reported 535 of its alumni were serving, and even tiny Austin College in Sherman claimed 43 alumni serving in the armed forces.[18]

Texans supported the war in myriad ways, and women played significant roles in nearly every aspect of this support. They demonstrated their commitment to the war effort in spite of the political and social constraints of the day, which placed boundaries on their participation in many aspects of life, including the right to vote. "All of the work is not done out where the marching ends—ah! No indeed—some of the biggest, bravest, greatest battles of any war are fought at home by the women, who, with breaking hearts and numberless tasks and burdens added to their original share of life's work, do their part," noted the *Houston Post*. While they could not serve in the military, many women supported the military as nurses or took certain jobs in industry and agriculture. As many as 449 Texas women served as army or navy nurses during the war, and at least seven of them died during the influenza epidemic that struck many parts of the world in the fall and winter of 1918. Those not serving in a medical capacity with the military, however, found numerous other ways to support the war. Women participated across the spectrum in wartime Texas and worked in the training camps, volunteered with the Red Cross, sought to eliminate alcohol and prostitution, participated in Liberty Loan campaigns, and organized food conservation efforts. The *Houston Post* urged women to "rise to the occasion," and they did so by the thousands. In 1918, the University of Texas hosted a "War College for Women" that drew nearly one hundred participants from volunteer organizations across the state who discussed numerous aspects of women's participation in, and support of, the war effort.[19]

Minorities also played an important part in the war, although they too were marginalized and oftentimes the objects of fear and suspicion who occasionally had their loyalty and patriotism challenged. Neither African Americans nor Hispanics were treated fairly during the war.[20] Nevertheless, the state's black communities showed their support of the war effort. Groups such as the Negro Patriotic League bolstered support on the home front, and quite a few African Americans served in the military to demonstrate their right to be considered full members of society. African American soldiers firmly believed that wearing the uniform entitled them to equal treatment in society. However, racial tensions in Texas remained strong and reached a boiling point in Houston during the summer of 1917.[21]

African Americans who could not serve in the military supported the war by holding rallies and patriotic meetings at local churches and schools and often invited white residents to attend. In Cleburne, just south of Fort Worth, black residents held a meeting at the local school during which as many as three hundred children sang southern folk songs. The local paper reported that a "special invitation is extended to the white people of the city for whom special seats will be arranged." In other places, such as Wichita Falls, the African American population held a "creditable and inspiring patriotic rally," which had been staged to quell rumors of "German propagandists working among the Negroes." In one speech, the president of the Negro Patriotic League was quoted as saying that "the Negroes of 1917 were just as true and loyal to their country as was the case in the sixties," referring to the Civil War.[22]

Although black expressions of patriotism and loyalty were accepted and considered part of the enthusiastic support of the war effort by many of the state's white residents, other incidents showed just how far Texas (and the nation) still had to go. In August 1917, racial tensions between African American soldiers and white residents in Houston were strained to the breaking point. Known as the Houston Riot, problems began with the construction of Camp Logan, one of the thirty-two training camps built by the U.S. Government to train National Guardsmen and draftees for the war. In the summer of 1917, while Camp Logan was under construction, the army ordered elements of the black Twenty-Fourth Infantry Regiment, then stationed in New Mexico, to Houston and Waco to guard both Camps Logan and MacArthur respectively, to prevent the theft of construction materials. In Waco, tensions flared when police got into a scuffle with black soldiers who had blocked a road outside a theater. That incident left several men injured, and several black soldiers were arrested. In response to the events in Waco, Brigadier General James Parker, commander of the U.S. Army's Southern Department, ordered that all soldiers had to have a signed pass from their commander to leave camp. He also stated that "Colored troops were sent to the Waco cantonment on the assurances of the Chief of Police that they would receive impartial treatment. As one tenth of all soldiers raised for this war in the United States will be colored, all patriotic citizens owe them kindly treatment." While tensions eased in Waco, they grew worse in Houston.[23]

Indeed, the Waco incident paled in comparison to the events in Houston several weeks later. Upon their arrival in Houston, black soldiers became the subject of extensive racial discrimination from locals, including the white construction workers in the camp. As mentioned earlier, many of the soldiers believed their status as United States soldiers entitled them to better treatment. However, some city officials feared that if black soldiers received equal treatment, the local African American population of Houston would demand something similar. Simply put, city officials were afraid to protect the black soldiers. While many of the black soldiers simply lived with their frustration, others did not.[24]

The tension boiled over on August 23, 1917, when two Houston policemen arrested a black soldier for interfering with the arrest of a black woman. A black military policeman, Corporal Charles Baltimore, sought information on the soldier's arrest but was instead beaten by city police. He managed to escape, but the Houston policemen fired their weapons at him and gave chase, eventually catching him and taking him to a police station. Although he was soon released, rumors swirled among his fellow soldiers at Camp Logan that he had been killed. Other soldiers wanted to go to the police station to find out if Baltimore was still alive and to secure his release. As tensions increased during the day, the white battalion commander ordered all weapons and ammunition to be secured. At that moment, a soldier cried out that a white mob was on its way to the camp. In response, approximately one hundred black soldiers grabbed their rifles and, under the control of Sergeant Vida

Henry, left Camp Logan and marched into Houston. Over a two-hour period, the soldiers killed fifteen white residents, including four Houston policemen and an Illinois National Guard officer, and wounded twelve others. Four black soldiers were killed. As night fell, Sergeant Henry told the remaining soldiers that they should try and slip back into Camp Logan. He then committed suicide by shooting himself in the head.[25]

Following the riot, authorities placed Houston under a curfew and on August 25, 1917, the army ordered the black soldiers of the Twenty-Fourth Infantry back to Columbus, New Mexico. From November 1, 1917, through March 26, 1918, 118 black soldiers from Sergeant Henry's Company I were tried for mutiny and riot at Fort Sam Houston in San Antonio, and 110 were found guilty. Because the riot occurred when the United States was officially at war, the sentences were particularly severe. Nineteen soldiers were hanged and sixty-three received life terms in federal prison. In addition, two of the battalion's white officers faced a court-martial but the charges were dropped. Furthermore, no white civilians involved in the incident were ever brought to trial.[26]

In response to the Houston Riot, a prominent resident of Denton County, Alvin C. Owsley, who was also a member of the state Council of Defense and whose son was a member of the Texas National Guard, spoke against the "danger of Negro soldiers." Focusing on the Houston Riot, Owsley believed that arming black soldiers was a mistake. Although he conceded that African Americans could serve in the military, he believed they should be assigned only non-combat tasks such as "cooking, washing, handling baggage, and digging trenches." Owsley went so far as to promise the residents of Wichita Falls, where he was speaking, that all African American troops would soon be "removed from the state." As those words indicate, tensions over the Houston Riot remained high for months afterward, but as historian Robert V. Haynes wrote, the Houston Riot "was one of the saddest chapters in the history of American race relations. It vividly illustrated the problems that the nation struggled with on the home front during wartime." As historian Garna Christian pointed out, black soldiers believed "they had bought into the system with a social contract that promised them liberty in exchange for the protection of the state." Sadly, that was not to be the case for decades after the conclusion of World War I.[27]

African Americans were not alone among the state's ethnic groups to be affected by the Great War. A day after the war declaration, the mayor of Wichita Falls, A. H. Britain, spoke at a patriotic rally hosted by the city. His remarks touched on a topic that loomed large at the time and which has continued to draw interest of scholars: the presence of German Americans in dozens of cities and towns in the state and the way they were treated by native-born citizens. Mayor Britain's remarks could have been echoed in any number of municipalities across the state. Stating that he had German ancestry on his mother's side and English on his father's, Mayor Britain remained neutral prior to the declaration of war. But once war was declared, he argued, German Americans would "be found among the most staunch and loyal of American citizens." While many foreign-born residents of Texas supported the war, there were many others who believed that German Americans could not be trusted. Most things associated with Germany were suddenly anathema to many Texans.[28]

Concerns over loyalty were pervasive at both the state and national level. For example, in November 1917, the federal government prohibited all "enemy" and "ally of enemy" insurance companies from doing business in the United States, in part because of fears that these insurance companies were using their inspectors to gain information about various facilities in the country. In Texas, the Wilson administration's order effectively shut the doors on fourteen foreign insurance companies operating in the state. Other incidents were much less significant but caused a stir nonetheless. For example, in February 1918 the mayor and ten citizens of the town of Fayetteville, which is located between Austin and Houston, were arrested and charged with espionage for displaying the German flag at the Fayetteville German Club. The mayor pleaded that the flag was displayed by mistake. And although all but one of those arrested were born in the United States, they were held in Houston on bonds totaling $69,000 until their case could go to trial.[29]

Loyalty to the United States was believed to be paramount during the war. Those who appeared to be unsupportive or who were perceived as holding loyalties to another country were condemned and were often the victims of violence. Foreigners across Texas became the focus of fear and suspicion to the extent that food, towns, and even city streets with German names were changed to erase any traces of lineage to Germany. For example, sauerkraut became "liberty cabbage," the King William district (named for Prussian king Wilhelm I) in San Antonio was renamed in honor of General Pershing, and many more examples too numerous to list were commonplace during the war. Such attitudes led many foreigners to stress their loyalty to the nation, and many went out of their way to appear patriotic. One way they did so was by ensuring they registered for the draft. In Texas, 24,371 foreigners registered for the draft, most of whom were citizens of allied or neutral nations. But at least 732 enemy aliens registered as well as 1,270 citizens of nations described as "allies of enemy aliens" in Texas, and many of them served in the military. At Camp Travis trained a group of Chinese men, one of whom was described as an expert linguist who, in addition to ten Chinese dialects, was fluent in English, French, German, Italian, and Spanish. For those too old to register or serve in the military, other options to prove their patriotism included subscribing to Liberty Bonds, and one German resident in sparsely populated Foard County placed a sign in his car that said "America First." Likewise, Senator Sheppard took an opportunity in Congress to publicly praise the contributions of German Texans, observing that they would be "just as loyal and as true, as ready to give their life and treasure for American ideals, as other elements of our citizenship."[30]

Suspicion of foreigners also led to fears of espionage and sabotage that spread quickly across Texas. This attitude was not unique to Texas, as the same sentiments drove the Espionage Act and the Trading with the Enemy Act through Congress during this period. These pieces of legislation were used to attempt to control foreigners and dissidents, and the legacy of those acts remains controversial to this day. Attitudes towards foreigners was strongly negative from the very beginning of the war. For example, on the day the United States declared war on Germany, Wilson's attorney general, Texan Thomas Watt Gregory, ordered the arrest of sixty alleged German plotters, all of whom were German nationals. The Justice Department accused each of the individuals of participating in "German intrigue" within the United States. Such attitudes at the national level reinforced fears of sabotage and espionage, particularly in Texas, where many residents believed that German spies moved at will across the Mexican border. Most rumors concerning German spies were false, but the fear and concern they engendered was real and affected many Texans. Furthermore, this fear encompassed not only foreigners but included those who were opposed to the war in general and the selective service draft.[31]

While rumors of German intrigues and sabotage occurred across the state, the Panhandle was particularly rife with rumors. Rumors swirled that the Amarillo police, in concert with law enforcement from Oklahoma and New Mexico, had captured German spies in possession of "maps and sketches of Amarillo and the Panhandle." However, a follow-up story in the same paper quoted the local police as saying they had no knowledge of spies being arrested. Nevertheless, the Amarillo newspaper continued to circulate reports of German spies moving through the area, while an Oklahoma newspaper editor was convinced that "German plotters" were active in the Texas Panhandle. Those rumors did not subside until the newspaper admitted that local law enforcement held no one under suspicion of "underhand work toward the government."[32]

Still, some residents of Amarillo and other Texas locales remained nervous. In Amarillo, the chief of police claimed the U.S. attorney general had ordered him to confiscate the weapons and ammunition of all foreign residents in Potter County. This order had supposedly been sent to all police chiefs in the state and caused much confusion. According to the chief of police, efforts to confiscate such weapons were "not an affront to aliens who have been making good inhabitants of Amarillo," but rather was a "precautionary measure" to prevent "unscrupulous" foreigners from starting a "small revolt or riot." At the time, there appeared to be no question as to whether this law violated any rights of the individual. However, the Wichita Falls chief of police went on record stating that his department had received no such orders form the attorney general. He did, however, claim to have received orders from the U.S. Marshals Service to arrest foreign-born citizens who by "word or deed," gave indications they were "alien enemies." The announcement of those orders fueled speculation that German residents of Wichita County would soon be arrested. While no arrests appeared to have been made because of that order, the *Wichita Daily Times* reported that some residents were indeed "alien enemies" by virtue of President Wilson's war proclamation, specifically those who had not been naturalized. Accordingly, those who were not naturalized and failed to complete the process would not be allowed to own firearms, ammunition, or "cipher-codes," and could be subject to "severe restrictions." The paper concluded by warning that it was an inopportune time to "cuss" the United States government.[33]

Incidents of suspicion occurred across the state. Stories circulated in El Paso of twelve Germans who were being held in the Fort Bliss jail. Other tales told of Germans who had crossed into Mexico, one of whom was a photographer who had snapped pictures of military fortifications. Authorities also arrested a Swiss woman in El Paso and charged her with violating the Espionage Act because she had allegedly attempted to "obtain military information from soldiers of the border patrol district." While there were many violent incidents along the border during the war, in many cases Mexican and U.S. law enforcements officers did cooperate with each other. In one case in the summer of 1917, at the height of espionage fears, two German citizens who were being held at Laredo escaped into Mexico. Caught by Mexican police, they were brought back to the United States where a law enforcement official described them as "dangerous enemies of the United States" who "might have made their ultimate escape and continued their plotting." In another example, this time in Dallas, U.S. Department of Justice officers charged a man with espionage because he carried maps of the Texas and Pacific Railway from Dallas to El Paso. The maps, written in German, included "various bridge locations in detail; a complete series of railroad and highway bridge maps in the Rio Grande country; blueprints showing the forts and military posts along the coast and border, and roads leading to the United States from Mexico." The man admitted to being German, but claimed he was simply on a "pleasure hike through Texas." If such was the case, his timing left much to be desired. Near Houston, the *Post* reported that three trestle bridges on tracks belonging to the Galveston, Harrisburg and San Antonio Railway Company had been set on fire in the days just prior to the war declaration. That act of sabotage spurred the company to post armed guards along its railroad.[34]

In other parts of Texas, rumors about spies and sabotage continued. In Abilene, the local newspaper described two attempts to blow up a railroad bridge just before the declaration of war. In nearby Cisco, authorities were concerned about a foreigner who did not live there and seemed unable to explain why he was there.

This stoked fears that the city's water supply might be in danger and fifty young men of the local home guard unit began a twenty-four-hour watch. Approximately one hundred miles to the east of Abilene, residents of Cleburne feared sabotage and spies because of the city's railroad network. As the local newspaper asserted, "There is no doubt about there being spies here at this time who are keeping posted on every move and every item that would be of value." While many of the spy fears dissipated as the summer wore on, the Cleburne paper insisted that spies were in the city as late as September 1917, stating "there are German spies right here in Cleburne. It is the duty of every liberty-loving American to keep close watch on all suspicious characters, and if possible give any suspicious characters close scrutiny." To the northwest, in the small town of Quanah the local newspaper refused to reprint speeches from a recruiting rally because of the possible presence of German spies in the area.[35]

Many fears of espionage centered on Germans crossing into the United States from Mexico. Such fears about the motives of German residents in Mexico were not completely unfounded, as the Zimmermann Telegram suggests. However, many Mexicans expressed sentiments in favor of the Allies, and some went so far as to hope that the Mexican government would declare war on Germany and confiscate German assets within the country. While one prominent Mexican observer noted that although his country could not send troops to European battlefields, they could "make Mexico safe for the allied nationals and for their properties. We can show our sympathy with the same cause for which we have been fighting for the last six years by aiding the Allies in every way, even though we are unable to assist materially in the war."[36] Such efforts, contemporary sources claimed, could easily help end "the wholesale traffic in ammunition, cattle smuggling, gun running," and other illegal activities along the border. To further strengthen this spirit of cooperation, the United States hosted the first ever Pan-American International Labor Conference at Laredo in November 1918, just as the armistice went into effect.[37] The conference attendees included U.S. Secretary of Labor William B. Wilson, famous labor leader Samuel Gompers, and representatives from Mexico and several Central and South American countries. Several months prior to the conference the Texas government had brokered an arrangement with Mexican authorities to allow Mexican citizens to enter the country to work on farms, railroads, and in coal mines for the duration of the war.[38]

One of the responses to these fears of espionage was the creation of official "home guards" to protect infrastructure in the United States. The federal government eventually established official home guard units. Secretary of War Newton Baker directed the Chief of the Militia Bureau, Major General Jesse M. Carter, to establish formal units to guard infrastructure and facilities across the country. Under the control of the Militia Bureau, the United States Guards organized their first unit in San Francisco in December 1917. Other units soon sprang up across the nation, although most were not formed until 1918. Military officials believed these United States Guards should be locally recruited through the volunteer process. However, during the spring of 1918, army officials realized that they had access to many draftees and other men who had been trained at one of the nation's thirty-two training camps, but for one reason or another could not join the American Expeditionary Force (AEF) in France. These men were transferred to the U.S. Guards as well.[39]

In Texas, the U.S. Army organized seven battalions of U.S. Guards, each with 31 officers and 602 enlisted men for a total of nearly 4,500 officers and men. Five of the battalions were on active service while two remained in reserve. They were located at Fort Sam Houston and Camp Stanley near San Antonio and Fort Bliss and Camp Cotton near El Paso, with detachments at Freeport, Galveston, Orange, Port Arthur, Beaumont, Houston, and Marfa. As indicated by their locations, most of these units were based along the border and the coast, where they provided security at shipyards, docks, railroad terminals, railroad bridges and tunnels, and other types of infrastructure and facilities. The U.S. Guards were demobilized in early 1919, several months after the armistice. Nevertheless, the presence of the U.S. Guards was significant. They filled an important gap in domestic security during the war that ad-hoc veterans' groups or informal "home guards" could never do. Furthermore, the U.S. Guards provided another outlet for men who wanted to participate in the war effort but were unable, for various reasons, to serve with the AEF in Europe.[40]

Texans had responded to the nation's declaration of war with a number of patriotic efforts. They served in home guards or contributed their time to the Red Cross and councils of defense. The U.S. Army created the United States Guards to provide defense on the home front—something that seemed crucial at a time rife with fears of rampant espionage. To enlist the thousands of men needed to prosecute the war in Europe, however, the armed forces would have to call on Texas's proud volunteer tradition, and more controversially, to conscript troops from the Lone Star State and throughout the nation.

# Chapter 4

# RAISING AN ARMY

On April 1, 1917, the U.S. Army consisted of 213,557 officers and men, a force that could hardly be expected to make an impact on the Western Front. Remarkably, though, less than two years later when the war ended with the November 1918 Armistice, the U.S. Army had grown to 3,685,458 men, of which 2,180,296 had been drafted into service, approximately 59 percent of the total. While the U.S. government had been extremely successful in building this army, the method by which it did so was controversial. While Texans across the state generally supported the declaration of war against Germany, debate on the selective-service draft proved far more contentious.[1]

The conscription debate raged from the halls of Congress to state capitals across the country. Would the United States be better served by relying on volunteers to build an army or should the country draft the manpower it needed? This was not a new issue; in the years prior to the war it had been discussed in relation to the Preparedness Movement. In fact, after the sinking of the *Lusitania* in 1915, President Wilson considered a "reorganization and expansion" of the military, although he hoped to avoid the impression that the United States might intervene in Europe. The president's deliberations spurred debate over volunteerism or the draft. And as late as February 1917, volunteerism appeared to be the preferred method to raise an army.[2]

In March, however, Secretary of War Newton Baker admitted that a draft might be necessary if volunteerism failed to provide the requisite manpower. As intervention became more certain by early 1917, President Wilson put his support behind the effort to pass the Selective Service Bill. Debate raged in Congress, in the media, and in communities across the nation. Texas congressmen contributed in significant ways to the national discussion.[3]

In the Senate, Morris Sheppard came out in favor of the draft, arguing that it would create an army by "quiet, orderly, and intelligent selection," rather than an army based on patriotism alone. In the House, Thomas L. Blanton offered his perspective to Congress on April 26, 1917. Representing the Panhandle and Southern Plains, Blanton expressed his support for the draft in a speech that was widely circulated across his wide West Texas district. While Blanton represented the consensus view that supporting the president meant supporting the draft, not all Texas congressmen agreed. Tom Connally recalled that he and Daniel E. Garrett were on "opposite sides of the draft bill when the question first popped up." In fact, Garrett entered numerous telegrams and letters into the *Congressional Record* from constituents who both supported and opposed the draft. When Garrett spoke in Congress, as Connally remembered, he discussed the merits of the volunteer system but ended his speech in support of the draft.[4]

Texans were more divided on the draft issue than they had been on the war declaration, and many, if not most Texans, appeared to favor volunteerism. For example, one letter to Congress from a citizen in Port Arthur read, "No state or nation has ever done more than Texas to withstand tyranny and maintain her rights by the sword, and the history of her volunteer army is the brightest in the world . . . If Texans are to do their best fighting, they prefer to go voluntarily." One day after war was declared, the *Houston Post* carried an article with the headline, "Texas could muster army of million if called upon."[5] Others, however, ardently supported the draft: "You are not reflecting the sentiment of the people of Texas in opposing President Wilson's selective conscription plan . . . The people of this community favor the selective-conscription bill as proposed by President Wilson," read a petition to the Texas congressional delegation from Wichita Falls. In El Paso, a group of businessmen wrote Senator Sheppard that they stood "squarely behind our President in demanding respect for our flag, both on land and sea, and we believe in universal compulsory military training, and we urge you to use all the power of your high office in passing a bill embodying this principle." In San Antonio, more than two hundred businessmen, in conjunction with that city's mayor, planned a letter to Texas's congressional delegation asking them to vote in favor of universal military training. While many of the state's political leaders fondly recalled the state's long tradition of volunteerism that began in the Texas Revolution and continued through the Civil War, most soon realized that volunteers simply could not provide the manpower the nation would need during the war. However reluctantly, then, the state's political leaders came to endorse the Selective Service Bill. Representative James C. Wilson typified this attitude, writing that because he was the "son of a volunteer who went out at the first call of the south and staid [*sic*] four years at the front, I approached this subject with a natural prejudice against conscription." But after listening to the debates on conscription he too came out in favor of the draft and in later years recalled with pride his vote for the draft bill.[6]

The only Texas congressman who refused to vote for the Selective Service Bill was no stranger to controversy. Once again, Jeff McLemore voted in opposition to his colleagues and argued that conscription would lead to militarism. His views on the matter led him to speculate that "propagandists" from New York City were behind the U.S. intervention in the war. McLemore went so far as to argue that the letters and telegrams he received in support of the draft had been created by this propaganda machine. As he stated, "Can you imagine anything more impudent than this New York propaganda . . . dictating to the people of Texas what to do?" McLemore also correctly pointed out that Texans were divided in their opinions about the draft, stating that Texas business owners supported the draft while agricultural interests and farmers tended to favor the volunteer system. Applauded by the House of Representatives, McLemore concluded his speech by stating that the draft would perpetuate a military system that he believed would result in the "end of our republican form of government." Nevertheless, while it was true that Texans, like many in the nation, believed in the virtues of a volunteer system, the realities of the war in Europe soon convinced most Texans that a draft was the most appropriate way to raise an army of the size necessary to make a difference in the war. Once Texans decided to support the draft, they did so enthusiastically. The Texas Senate passed a resolution by nineteen votes to two that endorsed the Selective Service Bill, while the Texas House debated a resolution that "unemployed and unproductive" individuals should be the first to be called. That resolution was never approved.[7] By late spring 1917, the bill had met with approval from both houses of Congress, and President Wilson signed the Selective Service Act on May 18. The first registration was scheduled for June 5. Those who wanted to volunteer would still have ample opportunity to do so, although the draft would be the chief source of manpower for the war.

The state's chief executive during the draft debates, Governor Ferguson, initially remained committed to the volunteer system and expressed his views in a letter to Representatives Sam Rayburn and Daniel Garrett, both of whom served on the House Military Affairs Committee. In his letter, Ferguson argued conscription was unnecessary "as far as Texas is concerned" because, he believed, the state could easily secure 500,000 Texas National Guardsmen as volunteers. He also went so far as to say, "I doubt if any large amount of volunteers could be obtained if it was known that our boys were to enlist under officers unknown to them. All of our boys in Texas want to enlist under officers appointed in Texas." In response, Rayburn suggested that the governor take up the issue with the secretary of war. While it was true that the National Guard would play an important role during World War I, even that institution could never provide the equivalent manpower of the draft. As late as July 1917, after the draft had been implemented and the first registration had taken place, Ferguson and others members of his administration continued to speak out in favor of volunteering. For example, a spokesperson for the Texas Department of Labor issued a statement that conscription would pose a "serious handicap" to Texas farmers. In the end, however, Ferguson eventually came to favor the Selective Service and sent a telegram to President Wilson expressing his support.[8]

Federal officials wanted a decentralized and easy to implement program, so they specifically designed the draft to rely heavily on state and local government for administrative support. At the national level, the U.S. Army provost marshal, Major General Enoch Crowder, oversaw the selective service system while state governors were responsible for the draft within their states. Each state consisted of several districts, each of which was under the responsibility of a district board. Texas had four districts: Fort Worth, Houston, Austin, and Tyler. The district boards had two main purposes. First, they reviewed decisions by county-level boards; second, the district boards made all decisions regarding individual exemption claims for agricultural and industrial reasons. The district boards provided oversight of the county boards and tried to ensure objectivity. However, in early twentieth-century Texas, discrimination remained prevalent and black men tended to be drafted at a higher percentage than white men (37 versus 22 percent) in the state. While this was true overall, there were individual counties in which blacks and whites were drafted in closer to equivalent numbers, and as historian Robert Wooster observed, black men had limited opportunities to volunteer for the armed forces and thus a larger pool of them was available to be drafted.[9]

Hispanics were also drafted into the U.S. Army, although instances of discrimination against them were common. For example, the *San Antonio Express* reported that large numbers of men who had received their notices to report to the draft board for medical exams had failed to show up. The reason, the paper claimed, was because they were Mexicans and had gone back to their home country rather than be drafted into the army. On the other hand, the Mexican government also directed their ambassador to the United States to investigate complaints that Mexican nationals were being forced to join the U.S. Army. And while there was no evidence to support such allegations, a Mexican newspaper claimed that 10,000 Mexicans had been forced into the U.S. Army and that "President Wilson has ordered them sent to the front before any other contingent."[10]

Because the Selective Service Act allowed state governors to appoint the members of local exemption boards, Governor Ferguson influenced the composition of some exemption boards in the state. In some cases, his appointments to local boards drew the unsurprising charge that he was playing politics. In fact, even General Crowder expressed his concern about the composition of Texas exemption boards because of the governor's choices. Crowder went so far as to state in a newspaper article that Governor Ferguson's recommendations had "caused the Provost Marshal General's Department more trouble than all the other states combined."

Indeed, some of Ferguson's selections were challenged, which did nothing but delay the operation of some local boards. Suspect board members were replaced, and the state published a final list of the initial board members for the Texas county boards in July 1917. By then June 5 had already come and gone. On that day the first national draft registration took place for all men between the ages of 21 and 30.[11]

Because the local boards had not been finalized by the first draft registration day, preparations for draft registration day fell to local government officials such as the sheriff and county clerk. Despite this obstacle, the first draft registration went off without a hitch in most Texas counties. In some, draft registration was accompanied by parades and patriotic displays, while in others the day was somber and businesslike. In Amarillo, many residents considered the parade held that day to be one of the "most stupendous" the city had ever seen. But in Cleburne, the local paper observed that draft registration day "passed very quietly." Whether local communities celebrated or not, the draft was overwhelmingly successful. In Fort Worth, a local editor noted, "Those in charge of the registration are well pleased with the results attained and with the apparent willingness of eligibles to come forward and enroll their names." In fact, the number of men who registered for the draft impressed a great many county officials, primarily because officials based their estimates on the number of men who paid taxes. On draft registration day, however, they found that far more men registered for the draft than had paid taxes, which perhaps was not an altogether pleasant surprise.[12]

Texas officials estimated that as many as 425,000 men might register in the state, while nationwide registrations were estimated at 10 million. As it turned out, 409,743 Texans signed on during the first registration, and of that number, 139,929 men were called for examination and 50,108 were accepted for military service.[13]

Although Texas authorities did not expect serious trouble with the draft registration, there were scattered incidents across the nation, and authorities remained vigilant in areas that were expected to have more resistance to the draft. In Wichita Falls, the sheriff fully expected trouble on registration day, although it did not materialize, while in Denton County authorities expressed concern about one part of the county because of "some evidence of disaffection and opposition to the selective draft registration." In nearby Dallas, anti-draft circulars surfaced that read "Down with conscription—refuse to register." Local authorities responded with extra vigilance on draft registration day. In East Texas, authorities arrested eighteen people in the town of Emory and confiscated a half-dozen rifles. According to a member of the sheriff's department, those arrested had held secret meetings and were "laying plans for an organized and armed resistance."[14]

By far the most significant example of draft resistance and opposition to the war in Texas came from the Farmers and Laborers Protective Association of America (FLPA). In May 1917, authorities arrested seven men in the West Texas town of Snyder on conspiracy charges. More arrest warrants brought in additional individuals in the area from Abilene to Wichita Falls, all of whom had ties to the FLPA, which had been established in 1915 with a stated purpose of strengthening cooperation between farmers and laborers. However, a small number of individuals attempted to use the association to foment draft resistance. Those men allegedly attempted to coerce other members into opposing the government, resisting the draft, and killing "on sight any conscription officer or officer of the army who should give him a gun with which to fight." Another man testified that they were told to "go when called, but to shoot down officers after they were armed and then return home."[15]

Eventually, more than fifty men were indicted on conspiracy charges, including FLPA state organizer G. T. Bryant. As more information about this alleged conspiracy surfaced, communities resorted to using local home guards to forestall trouble, and police officers killed one man who resisted arrest and opened fire on them. Finally, as the first draftees made their way to their training camps in early September 1917, fifty-six men charged with conspiracy were brought to trial. After a month-long trial with extensive media coverage, the jury found only three of the men guilty, including Bryant, FLPA state president Z. L. Risley, and secretary S. J. Powell. The court found them guilty of conspiring to "overthrow, put down and destroy by force the Government of the United States, and to levy war against them." Although each man proclaimed his innocence, all three received six-year sentences. The remaining defendants were either acquitted or had their cases dismissed. Nevertheless, the judge in the case admonished them all to "live and act" in such a way as to prove their loyalty to the United States.[16]

While the FLPA was the largest case of draft opposition in the state, other examples included two men in Atascosa County whom U.S. marshals arrested and charged with "obstructing and hindering recruiting and enlisting for the service of the United States." As one marshal reported, both men asked locals to resist the draft law and refuse to fight against Germany. One of the men was also charged with circulating false reports that engendered "disloyalty against the United States military service." Both men waived an initial hearing and posted bond, one at $5,000 and the other at $1,000, while waiting for a Grand Jury to convene in December 1917. Likewise, in San Antonio, the editor of the monthly magazine *Liberty* was arrested for obstructing the draft and held on a $5,000 bond. Finally, a twenty-year veteran U.S. Army bandleader stationed at Camp Travis in San Antonio received a thirty-year sentence for refusing to play the *Star-Spangled Banner* and later playing a German song at Fort Sam Houston.[17]

There were also incidents where men simply failed to register. In most cases, officials quickly concluded that the failure to register was unintentional, as many of the men who failed to register did so because they lived in isolated rural areas and either simply did not know about the draft, believed they were entitled to an exemption based on religious grounds, or because of a medical condition. However, others failed to register intentionally and appeared to have gotten away with it. Authorities attempted to bring those men, known as "slackers," to justice. Local authorities also advised men who had registered to always carry a copy of their registration form with them when they left the local area so they would not be mistaken for a slacker. In fact, it was not uncommon for police to stop men on the streets and ask for proof that they had registered, particularly if they were strangers. Law enforcement organizations across the state also held occasional "slacker round ups." In Fort Worth, for example, one of those "round ups" brought more than 1,200 men to City Hall, where authorities would determine if they had registered or not. Senior National Guard officers in the state also supported such roundups. Brigadier General Henry

Hutchings, for example, sent a telegram in mid-June 1917 to police departments across the state asking them to arrest and prosecute "slackers." This was not a small problem, as the government classified approximately 14,173 Texans as slackers after the first draft registration and call. This stands in stark contrast to the attitudes expressed by many Texans that their state would have no trouble raising the men needed to fight in Europe. Indeed, draft avoidance remained an issue in Texas throughout the war.[18]

The key to a successful implementation of the draft rested with the county level exemption boards, which is where the actual work of registering, selecting, examining, and sending men off to training camps took place. In the United States, there were 4,648 local boards with more than 14,000 members. In Texas, there were 280 exemption boards, one for every county and each city with a population greater than 30,000. Each board consisted of three members. One pertinent feature of the local boards was that the members were not military officers. Rather, the board members were members of the local community who understood the local situation, which purportedly allowed them to impartially choose who would be drafted. While women served on local Councils of Defense, they did not serve on draft boards during this time. In Texas, 841 men served on local boards during the war. Politicians and military leaders argued that the boards served as the link between the individual citizen and the federal government, and without a doubt the county exemption boards held significant power over the lives of local young men.[19]

Once draft registration was complete and the local boards were established, the process of organizing the draft registration records and giving each man a number began. Finally, on July 20, 1917, the first draft numbers were called in a national ceremony. Once the numbers had been drawn and posted, the local boards called the corresponding individuals in for medical examinations and to review requests for draft exemption. Those who requested an exemption would either have their request approved or forwarded to the district board for further review. Those whose exemption requests were ultimately rejected would then be certified for service. During the first draft registration period, Texans requested 67,769 exemptions, and the local boards granted 81 percent of those (55,253). Each local draft board employed the services of physicians and lawyers to help with processing the drafted men, and the medical exams were an important aspect of deciding whether men were qualified for service. In 1917 alone, Texas doctors examined 119,779 men for service and found 91,312 fit, which left 28,467 who were not. Those who passed were certified for military service by the board. Once a man had been certified for service, he received a date to report back to the board for induction into the army and for shipment to a training camp. The boards also used military instructors to teach the new draftees rudimentary military skills before they departed for training camp.[20]

The scale of the work the boards accomplished varied widely based on the size of the county. For example, the boards in Fort Worth and Tarrant County dealt with nearly 32,000 men after the first registration period, while the board in sparsely populated Foard County in Northwest Texas had to contend with just 1,200 registrants. One fourteen-county swath in North and Northwest Texas registered more than 88,000 men and inducted more than 10,000 of them into the army. To illustrate the effectiveness of the selective service system over volunteerism, a Texas National Guard regiment recruited over that same fourteen-county area yielded approximately 2,000 recruits. The number of draftees often vastly outnumbered the much slower volunteer process.[21]

While officials across the state worked to implement the draft through the summer of 1917, dozens of recruiters from the Regular Army, the Navy, and the Marine Corps sought to bolster their ranks with young Texas volunteers. One reason men joined the Regular Army was because they often had more options than the infantry. For example, a man could join the fledgling Air Service, the Quartermaster Corps, the Signal Corps, or another branch that required unique skills. The consensus at the time was that a man who volunteered had more control over his fate. If he waited to be drafted, he could easily end up where the army thought it best to place him, surrounded by strangers.[22]

U.S. Army plans called for the service to have 1,580,000 men in uniform by the beginning of September 1917. But in early July, the army was a long way from that goal, with only 247,000 men in the ranks. At the same time, the U.S. Navy had 128,389 personnel while the U.S. Marine Corps stood at 30,000. The entire National Guard consisted of approximately 300,000 men and officers. With those goals in mind, army, navy, and marine recruiters set up offices in most of the state's major cities and traveled into the state's more remote areas on recruiting trips. The military services used all the techniques available to them to recruit men and were not shy about relying on famous names from the past to draw recruits. For example, in Amarillo, Captain Fitzhugh Lee, a member of the U.S. Cavalry and a grandson of Confederate General Robert E. Lee, spent a week recruiting volunteers to attend the first officers' training camp in Leon Springs near San Antonio. When he left, he had convinced ninety-three men to apply for the camp. During the week that Captain Lee spent in Amarillo, the city saw twenty-one men join the army and fourteen join the navy. Farther east, in Vernon, eighteen men had joined the army and thirty the navy by the end of June 1917. Into the summer of 1917, Fort Worth had provided the army with 427 men, the navy with 424, and the marines with 74 recruits. During the war, more than 19,000 Texans served with the U.S. Navy, and two of them, James O. Richardson and Chester W. Nimitz, would later command the U.S. Pacific Fleet prior to and during World War II.[23] The army reached the milestone of 200,000 volunteer recruits on August 27, 1917, but it was simply not enough to build an army of the size needed to make a difference on the Western Front, and many recruiters hoped that the draft would spur men to volunteer before they were conscripted.[24]

As army and navy recruiters scoured the state for volunteers and local officials worked to implement the draft, some men turned to another option: the Texas National Guard. The National Guard played an important role in the Texan experience of the war, par-

CHART 1: This chart shows the number of men recruited by the Regular Army during the early months of the war. SOURCE: *New York Times*, May 8, June 3, July 1, August 8, September 5, 1917.

| Date | Nationwide | Texas |
|---|---|---|
| May 7, 1917 | 53,012 | 2,395 |
| June 1, 1917 | 94,623 | 3,674 |
| July 1, 1917 | 131,623 | 4,704 |
| August 7, 1917 | 180,766 | 6,134 |
| September 4, 1917 | 203,954 | 7,161 |

ticularly because it represented the volunteer tradition of men from local communities forming a unit to serve overseas. As a recruiting poster used in Wichita Falls attested, men who joined the National Guard would serve with officers and men from their own communities and would "receive the attention, love and respect of the people at home." One poster ended with a famous flourish: "Be a 'went' instead of a 'sent'—if you must go sooner or later, why not go with the boys from home?"[25]

While the militia tradition in the United States has a long and storied history, efforts to professionalize the National Guard did not occur until the early twentieth century with the passage of the 1903 Dick Act. In early 1917, the National Guard had an authorized strength of 180,000, although its numbers were well below that. On the positive side, many of its members had gained recent military experience on the border with Mexico, where 112,000 guardsmen served between 1916 and 1917 after President Wilson mobilized them in support of General Pershing's expedition to capture Pancho Villa. In early 1917, the Texas contribution to the border mobilization consisted of the Sixth Separate Brigade, commanded by General Hutchings. The brigade included the Second, Third, and Fourth Texas Infantry regiments as well as the First Cavalry Squadron and various engineer, artillery, and hospital units, a total of 4,755 men, most of whom were ready to go home by early 1917 and were in the process of demobilization.[26]

With the public release of the Zimmermann Telegram in February 1917, the Texas National Guard suspended its demobilization. On March 21, 1917, approximately two weeks before Congress declared war on Germany, National Guard leaders called the Second, Third, and Fourth Infantry Regiments back to active duty. When the United States declared war on Germany, the *Houston Post* astutely observed, "The value of the training on the border of Mexico is going to be apparent now. The country questioned the need of that experience. It will question no more. Those 150,000 troops of the National Guard are as ready for war today as is the regular army. Added to the 120,000 of which the regular army is composed, they form a force of 370,000 men—examples of preparedness in its best form."[27]

Over the spring and summer of 1917, the National Guard focused on recruiting to reach its new goals. In Austin, General Hutchings and Governor Ferguson developed plans to raise 12,000 new troops in seventy-three units and four new regiments. The expansion called for a reorganization of the Texas National Guard that included two infantry brigades of three regiments each, one separate infantry regiment, as well as a cavalry regiment, two regiments of artillery, and one battalion each of field engineers and Signal Corps. The regiments with border service (Second, Third, and Fourth Infantry) became the First Brigade under the command of Brigadier General John A. Hulen. General Hutchings assumed command of the Second Brigade, which included the newly organized First, Fifth and Sixth Infantry Regiments. The separate infantry regiment, the Seventh, would be under the command of Colonel Alfred Wainwright Bloor, a forty-one-year-old Austin attorney who had served with the Texas National Guard since the Spanish-American War and who had been on border service with the Sixth Separate Brigade. One of the men on Bloor's staff was Major William Culberson, a relative of Senator Culberson. Governor Ferguson and Adjutant General Hutchings approved commissions for 417 new officers, while General Hulen managed the statewide recruiting effort.[28]

The first task of the new National Guard officers was to recruit their companies in specific areas of the state. Carrying a set of instructions from General Hulen, these officers fanned out across the state. Some had spent years in the National Guard or came from distinguished military families and had prior experience with the U.S. Army in Cuba and the Philippines during the Spanish-American War. Others, however, were recent graduates of the first Officers Training Camp at Leon Springs. Regardless, those officers needed to secure the cooperation of prominent citizens as well as local officials and newspapers if they planned to succeed in recruiting the Texas National Guard to full strength.[29]

Each county in the state had received a draft quota based on the number of men who had registered in that location, although the number of men who volunteered for service with the National Guard, Army, or Navy prior to draft day was subtracted from the quota. For example, if a county had a quota of 200 men and 50 had already joined the military, the draft quota would be reduced to 150. Because there were still some who believed that the draft system was not the right way to raise an army, General Hulen specifically directed his National Guard officers not to use the word "conscript" when referring to draftees, and later, 90th Division commander General Henry T. Allen was quoted as saying that there was no reason to call a man who waited to be drafted any less of a patriot than someone who volunteered. That did not keep Hulen, however, from stressing to his officers that they could direct the attention of prospective recruits to any "special advantage that may be claimed for any particular unit or arm of the service."[30]

Because many Texans rhetorically embraced the volunteer tradition, most National Guard officers expected Texas men to flock to the colors, and they stressed that connection with the past to help them recruit men. Surprisingly, however, the number of volunteers initially did not meet expectations. Recruiting posters plastered across the state said such things as, "Don't be drafted, Volunteer in the National Guard of Texas . . . don't be a slacker. Your friends around you are all going. What are you going to do? Get into line and answer the bugle call!" Another poster asked young men to think of the future: "In after years, don't let your children be embarrassed when they are asked, 'where was your father in 1917?'" Such posters, however, appeared to be less effective than hoped.[31]

Several newspapers published a plea from General Hulen in which he wrote, "Texas needs 12,000 men. She must have them . . . young men of Texas must maintain the honor of the commonwealth for which their forefathers died." Another Texas National Guard officer, Colonel Oscar Guessaz, summed up the pressure to join the National Guard, writing that the "men of Texas should hide their faces in shame, if they permit the call of the National Guard to go unanswered." As it turned out, this push for recruits was successful, and Texas was lauded for the number of recruits secured. In fact, National Guard leaders highlighted Wichita Falls as a paragon of recruiting, when efforts there resulted in 310 volunteers to fill two companies. General Hulen sent a congratulatory telegram to local officers and called the city an "inspiration to the rest of the state." Thus, by the time the first draft numbers were called on July 20, 1917, the Texas National Guard had recruited thousands of volunteers to serve in its ranks. As one Oklahoma chaplain who served with many Texans on the Western Front summed up these Texas volunteers, they were "big hearted because they had a big state with a big history back of them; ready to lay down life, for their forefathers had sacrificed when Texas was a Republic within itself." While most of those young Texans probably believed that they would serve with others from their communities in the National Guard, most were also likely not fully cognizant of the significance of the fast approaching federalization of the National Guard, scheduled for August 5, 1917, which meant that they would no longer be under the control of the states.[32]

During the remainder of the war, there were two additional draft registration days, one in June 1918 and a third in September 1918. By the third registration, the federal government allowed those who had registered for the draft to volunteer for the navy or marines. The draft boards were further ordered to provide men to those branches if voluntary enlistments did not fill the need. In total, 127,797 Texans were drafted into the army during the war. Alongside 37,704 volunteers for the Regular Army and National Guard, as well 16,889 volunteers for the U.S. Navy and 2,073 who joined the Marines, a grand total of 184,463 Texans served in the military during World War I.[33]

Recruiting efforts embraced the entire community and were an important part in the life of thousands of Texans across the state. The presence of recruiters, the many patriotic recruiting rallies, and the sight of young Texans enlisting in the various military branches brought the war home in ways that nothing else could. For many Texans, seeing a soldier walking down the street was as close as they would ever come to the Western Front. With recruiting and the draft in full swing by the late summer of 1917, work continued to progress on the training camps that were being built to house and train these thousands of soldiers from Texas and other states. Until the training camps were ready, recruits remained in their local communities through the hot, dry Texas August. Throughout 1917 and 1918, military training camps sprouted all over Texas, leaving an indelible mark on the state's landscape.

The Temptation, *Dallas Morning News*, March 1, 1917.

No More Men Are Needed for
the Watch on the Rhine, but
# 26,000 Men Are Wanted
to Relieve the
## Watch on the Rio Grande

This 1917 recruiting poster shows that the U.S.–Mexico border figured prominently in American security concerns during the World War-I era. Poster drawn by
Gordon Grant. From https://www.loc.gov/resource/ppmsca.39708/ [Accessed June
21, 2017]. *Library of Congress Prints and Photographs Division, Washington, D.C.*

# NO WAR TALK!

## Attorney General Gregory, says:

# 'OBEY THE LAW

# Keep Your Mouth Shut!"

No War Talk! An example of the government's efforts to prevent criticism of the war in order to keep spies from overhearing sensitive information. From https://www.loc.gov/item/2002695593/ [accessed July 27, 2018]. *Library of Congress Prints and Photographs Division, Washington, D.C.*

## AUSTIN

Austin during WWI. A view of the state capital during the war. *Photo Courtesy of the Texas Military Forces Museum, Camp Mabry, Austin, Texas.*

The "Fighting Mechanics" Band from Camp Mabry, in Austin. *Photo Courtesy of the Texas Military Forces Museum, Camp Mabry, Austin, Texas.*

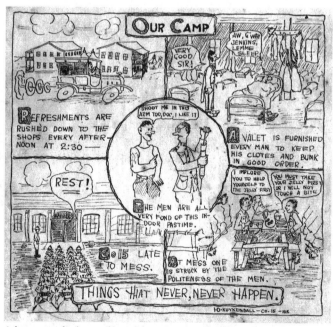

A humorous look at military life at Camp Mabry during the war. Camp Mabry was used primarily to train mechanics. *Photo Courtesy of the Texas Military Forces Museum, Camp Mabry, Austin, Texas.*

The cover of a souvenir photo album for soldiers stationed at Camp Bowie, Fort Worth, Texas. *Photo Courtesy of the Texas Military Forces Museum, Camp Mabry, Austin, Texas.*

Soldiers at Fort Worth's Camp Bowie faced a severe winter in 1917–18. Conditions were exacerbated by a lack of winter clothing; however, these soldiers appear to be warm in their overcoats. *Photo Courtesy of the Texas Military Forces Museum, Camp Mabry, Austin, Texas.*

Officers and men of the Love Field Aviation School posing for a panoramic photo in 1918. Texas had the most training fields for the fledgling air service in the nation. *Photo Courtesy of the Texas Military Forces Museum, Camp Mabry, Austin, Texas.*

A typical Texas soldier? Private Eugene Long came from the Houston area and served with the 143rd Infantry Regiment of the 36th Division. *Photo Courtesy of the Texas Military Forces Museum, Camp Mabry, Austin, Texas.*

African American soldiers at Camp Travis, San Antonio. *Jesse Alexander Photograph Collection, Schomburg Center for Research in Black Culture, Photographs and Prints Division, New York Public Library; available online at https://digitalcollections.nypl.org/items/510d47e2-08c7-a3d9-e040-e00a18064a99 [Accessed Oct. 5, 2018].*

Adjutant Gen. Henry Hutchings. Born in England, Hutchings was a newspaper publisher in Austin and served as Adjutant General of the Texas National Guard from 1911–17. In 1917, he was mobilized and went overseas as commander of the 36th Division's 71st Brigade. *Photo Courtesy of the Texas Military Forces Museum, Camp Mabry, Austin, Texas.*

General John Hulen, a railroad executive, commanded Texas National Guard forces during the 1916 border mobilization and then served as commander of the 36th Division's 72nd brigade during the war. *Photo Courtesy of the Texas Military Forces Museum, Camp Mabry, Austin, Texas.*

General John Pershing reviewing Texas troops while he was serving as commander of the U.S. Southern Department in March, 1917. *Photo Courtesy of the Texas Military Forces Museum, Camp Mabry, Austin, Texas.*

The Reviewing stand for the major parade of the 36th Division through Fort Worth in April, 1918. Dignitaries included the governors of Texas and Oklahoma, and 36th Division Commander Major General Edwin Greble. *Photo Courtesy of the Texas Military Forces Museum, Camp Mabry, Austin, Texas.*

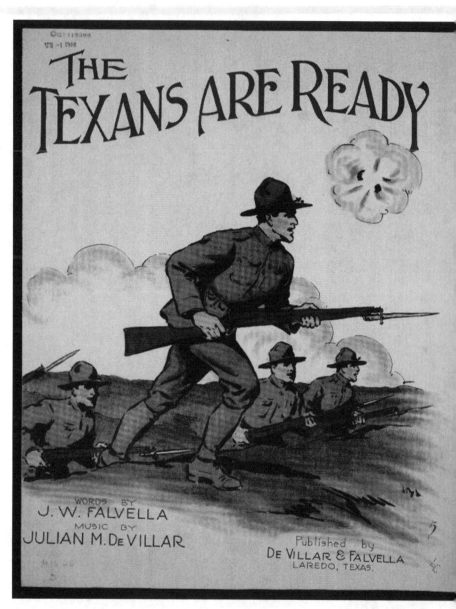

The cover for the sheet music to "The Texans Are Ready," which is an example of the belief prevalent among many at the time that Texas soldiers were some of the best in the country. From https://www.loc.gov/item/2013562485/[Accessed Oct. 9, 2018]. *Library of Congress Prints and Photographs Division, Washington, D.C.*

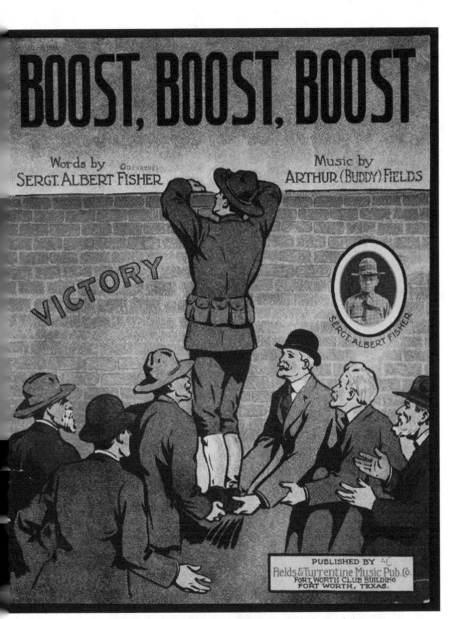

The cover of the sheet music to "Boost, Boost, Boost," which depicted the support
of local communities for their soldiers. In this case, civilians help boost a soldier
over a wall. From https://www.loc.gov/item/2013563278/[Accessed Oct. 9, 2018].
*Library of Congress Prints and Photographs Division, Washington, D.C.*

Colonel Alfred W. Bloor (front row, center), an Austin attorney, poses with the officers of the 142nd Infantry Regiment upon their return from France. Colonel Bloor was the only one of the 36th Division's four regimental commanders to remain with his regiment during the war. *Photo Courtesy of the Texas Military Forces Museum, Camp Mabry, Austin, Texas.*

General Hulen and the staff of the 72nd brigade in France with their French liaison officer. *Photo Courtesy of the Texas Military Forces Museum, Camp Mabry, Austin, Texas.*

An example of final training in France before moving to the front. Here, Texas soldiers of the 144th Infantry regiment practice shooting rifle grenades. Smoke from exploding grenades can be seen in the distance. *Photo Courtesy of the Texas Military Forces Museum, Camp Mabry, Austin, Texas.*

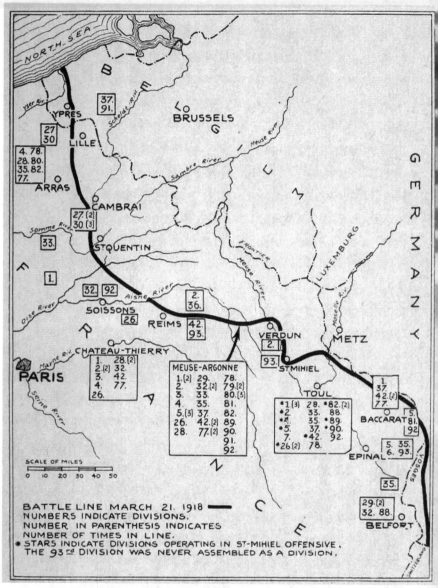

"WHERE AMERICAN DIVISIONS WERE IN LINE, FROM OUR ENTRY INTO THE TRENCHES UNTIL THE ARMISTICE." From Frederick Palmer, *Our Greatest Battle (The Meuse-Argonne)* (New York: Dodd, Mead, and Company, 1919), 14, <http://www.gutenberg.org/files/49205/49205-h/images/io31.jpg> [Accessed July 10, 2018]. The 36th Division is visible on the Aisne River north of Reims. The 90th is clumped together with several other divisions to the southeast of St. Mihiel.

Map of the Meuse-Argonne Offensive, Sept 26–Nov. 11, 1918. The Argonne
Forest and the Aisne River are visible in the lower left portion of the map. The
position of the 90th Division up to November 11, 1918, is visible in the vicinity
of the Meuse River and the town of Mouzay. From *Collier's New Encyclopedia*
(New York: P. F. Collier and Son, 1921), <https://commons.wikimedia.org/wiki/
File:Collier%27s_1921_World_War_-_Meuse-Argonne_offensive.jpg> [Accessed
July 10, 2018].

Lt. Emil Horner stands with Native American members of the 142nd Infantry, who used the Choctaw dialect to confuse Germans listening in on their transmissions. The Choctaw code talkers used their unique skills for the first time in the battle of Forest Farm, October 27, 1918. *Photo courtesy of the Texas Military Forces Museum, Camp Mabry, Austin, Texas.*

AEF commander General John J. Pershing decorates several members of the 36th Division after the Armistice. Note the unique Texas–Oklahoma arrowhead patch on the man's shoulder. *Photo courtesy of the Texas Military Forces Museum, Camp Mabry, Austin, Texas.*

A troop train decorated with graffiti from the 36th Division "Texas–Oklahoma" on the way home, 1919. *Photo courtesy of the Texas Military Forces Museum, Camp Mabry, Austin, Texas.*

A telegram from Private Eugene Long (see photo #10) letting his family in Houston know that he has made it back safely from France aboard the USS *Powhatan*, and that he was "feeling fine." *Photo courtesy of the Texas Military Forces Museum, Camp Mabry, Austin, Texas.*

Company L of the 141st Infantry, 36th Division, back from France in 1919. While there are a few smiles among the men, most are somber and serious and have the look of tired veterans. *Photo courtesy of the Texas Military Forces Museum, Camp Mabry, Austin, Texas.*

A 36th Division memorial is set up in Alamo Plaza, San Antonio, 1919, to celebrate the return of the state's National Guardsmen. The Alamo can be seen behind the arch. *Photo courtesy of the Texas Military Forces Museum, Camp Mabry, Austin, Texas.*

Corporal Samuel Sampler of the 36th Division, who received the Medal of Honor for his actions at the battle of Saint Etienne, October 8–10, 1918. *Photo courtesy of the Texas Military Forces Museum, Camp Mabry, Austin, Texas.*

Corporal Harold Turner, also of the 36th Division. He too received the Medal of Honor for his actions at the battle of Saint Etienne, October 8–10, 1918. *Photo courtesy of the Texas Military Forces Museum, Camp Mabry, Austin, Texas.*

*Chapter 5*

# TRAINING THE TROOPS

The U.S. military has long had a significant presence in Texas. The use of existing military facilities in Texas, in conjunction with a rapid expansion of military bases, was key to helping the state modernize and played an important role in the training of military personnel to serve on the Western Front. In fact, several of the military installations established in the state during World War I remain in use into the twenty-first century. To fully understand the role that Texas played in World War I, the relationship between the U.S. military and the state must be clearly understood.

The United States Army had been in Texas since the 1840s to guard the border with Mexico and to protect settlers from Indian attacks. Along the border, the army anchored its eastern line at Brownsville, its center at Laredo, and its western flank at El Paso. The location of forts shifted over time as the frontier pushed west. Although the army had maintained forces in Texas since the mid-nineteenth century, its presence in the early twentieth century had decreased but instability along the border kept U.S. forces nearby. The military presence in Texas centered on San Antonio and Fort Sam Houston, the headquarters for the United States Southern Department, which oversaw military forces stationed in Texas, New Mexico, Arizona, and Oklahoma.

One of the Southern Department's primary responsibilities was to patrol the border with Mexico. The department also supervised the organization of units for overseas service, oversaw National Guard mobilizations for units within the department, managed home guard battalions, and guarded significant utilities within Texas, New Mexico, and Arizona. When war broke out, Brigadier General John J. Pershing commanded the department, although he soon relinquished command to assume leadership of the American Expeditionary Forces (AEF). Brigadier General James Parker assumed command after Pershing, until he too left to serve in the AEF. For the remainder of the war, Major Generals John W. Ruckman, Willard A. Holbrook, and DeRosey C. Cabell all commanded the Southern Department at one time or another from San Antonio.[1]

Less than one month before the declaration of war in April 1917, the U.S. Army's First Provisional Infantry Division occupied sites across South Texas. Under the command of Brigadier General James Parker, the division's three infantry brigades and one artillery brigade, as well as supporting units, occupied posts at Camp Wilson and Fort Sam Houston in San Antonio and in Brownsville, Laredo, Eagle Pass, and Del Rio. Likewise, the Second Provisional Infantry Division occupied posts in West Texas, the Trans-Pecos region, and New Mexico. At the time, Brigadier General Edwin St. John Greble commanded the Second Division's artillery brigade. General Greble would play an important role in the formation of Texas National Guard troops at Fort Worth's Camp Bowie during the war. The First Provisional Cavalry Brigade also maintained its headquarters in El Paso, where it oversaw the operations of Colonel George T. Langhorne and his Eighth Cavalry Regiment, which patrolled the remote areas of the Big Bend region and Presidio County to prevent Mexican bandits from crossing into the United States.[2]

Although the war changed the composition of the forces along the border, the army maintained a consistent and significant force there throughout the war. In April 1917, the Southern Department rolls carried some 68,560 personnel. Nineteen months later, at the time of the November 1918 armistice, the department rolls carried almost the same number of officers and men: 68,325. At its highest point during the war, in May 1918, the Southern Department counted more than 101,000 soldiers. At its lowest point in May 1917, the department consisted of just over 53,000 troops. However, in keeping with the drawdown after the war, by September 1919 the Southern Department had become a shadow of its wartime strength as its rosters had dropped to just 23,986 officers and men. Nevertheless, this generally constant high level of troops in the department illustrated the importance ascribed to guarding the border in Texas, New Mexico, and Arizona during the war.[3]

The Southern Department's border patrol forces were divided

in five districts: Brownsville, Laredo, Eagle Pass, Big Bend, and El Paso. Each district contained small outposts scattered along the border. For example, the Brownsville District contained fifty-two outposts that stretched from Corpus Christi to Point Isabel. Each of the other districts contained similar numbers of outposts aimed at protecting infrastructure and crossing points along the border.[4]

The army also used several existing military forts and bases during the war. In addition to Fort Sam Houston, Austin's Camp Mabry saw continued service during the war, as did Camp Marfa in the Big Bend region. Likewise, Fort San Jacinto was one of the oldest military posts in Texas during World War I, having been first established during the Republic of Texas era in 1836. Spread over more than 1,500 acres, during World War I it served as a base for the defense of Galveston, as did the smaller Fort Travis, on Galveston's Bolivar Point. Interestingly, the Bolivar Point lighthouse could perhaps claim to be the only spot in Texas that suffered an artillery bombardment during the war. On November 16, 1917, gunners at nearby Fort San Jacinto accidently shelled the lighthouse, with one empty shell striking the lighthouse twenty-five feet above the base. Another shell landed in the front yard of a nearby house. Fortunately, no one was injured during the two-hour bombardment in which two dozen shells landed near the lighthouse. The shells had been intended to fall well short of the lighthouse into the water. Also along the coast, Fort Crockett, which had been established in 1897, served as the headquarters for the Coast Defenses of Galveston and was the site where the U.S. Army established its First Aero Squadron in 1913.[5] Fort Brown, near Brownsville, had been in operation since March 1846, and Fort Clark, near Brackettville, remained in use during the war as a border patrol base. El Paso's Fort Bliss also played an important role along the border, just as it had since its 1854 establishment. During the war, Fort Bliss became a center of military border patrol activities. Furthermore, the army established several temporary wartime camps associated with Fort Bliss, including Camp Courchesne for engineers, Camp Fort Bliss and Camp Owen Beirne for the cavalry, Camp Newton D. Baker for the Signal Corps, and Camp Stewart for Pennsylvania National Guard troops. Fort Bliss also hosted an officers' training school from May 15 to September 1, 1918. Other important permanent bases that supported border patrol activities included

Fort McIntosh, situated near Laredo in Webb County. Having been established in 1849, Fort McIntosh served as headquarters for the Laredo District of the border patrol. Finally, Fort Ringgold was also an older fort established near Rio Grande City in Starr County, from which border patrol operations were also carried out during the war.[6]

When the United States entered the war in April 1917, some of the first troops to depart for France included soldiers stationed in Texas. The U.S. Army's First Expeditionary Division, which later became the First Infantry Division, was created from troops that had been stationed along the U.S. and Mexican border, from Brownsville to El Paso and across New Mexico and Arizona. On May 24, 1917, just over six weeks after the declaration of war, the War Department began organizing them for overseas movement, and by June 3, 1917, the first contingent of troops for the new division had left the border for New Jersey to ship for France, where they arrived on June 26, 1917. On July 22, the second contingent left the border region and arrived in France on August 13, 1917. The last elements of the division, which included a field hospital from Fort Bliss, arrived in France on December 22, 1917.[7]

While existing facilities provided valuable infrastructure, there were simply not enough of them to handle the burgeoning U.S. Army. Thus, the expansion of military bases within the state provided a significant economic boost to the cities that were lucky enough to secure one. And although the military built all types of facilities, the centerpieces of the military expansion in Texas during World War I were arguably the four training camps that were built to house National Guardsmen and draftees as well as the creation of new flying fields for the army's nascent air arm. To ensure that the army had the room to train new recruits, thirty-two training camps were built in locations across the country to handle the influx of new soldiers. As one local paper noted, these "military cities" could house as many as 40,000 men each, and at the time there were fewer than 150 cities across the nation with populations that matched the camps. The magnitude of that effort was immense, and community leaders and politicians in Texas managed to secure four camps for the state.[8]

Of the thirty-two camps, sixteen were designed for National Guardsmen and sixteen for draftees. The main difference between them was that National Guard camps were built using more temporary structures while the draftee camps included more permanent structures because, the logic ran, the formers Guardsmen already had a modicum of military training and would not need to be in their camps as long as the draftees would, as they had no military training. Thus, in May 1917 Secretary of War Baker directed the departmental commanders to select the training camp sites. Because Texas fell within the purview of the Southern Department, the selection of camp locations fell to Brigadier General James Parker.[9]

San Antonio had the largest military presence of any city in the state, primarily because of Fort Sam Houston and the expansive training areas northwest of the city. Fort Sam Houston had been formally established in 1876, although the oldest military installation in the city was the San Antonio Arsenal, which had been used by the U.S. Army since 1859. However, in the summer of 1917, it was not at all clear that San Antonio would play such a large role in the military buildup. Officials in San Antonio were so convinced of their city's merits that they made no effort to secure one of the camps, believing their selection to host one of the training camps to train draftees and National Guardsmen was a foregone conclusion. As it turned out, the sentiments of city officials appeared to be true when San Antonio was, in fact, selected to host one of the camps. But, San Antonio's selection to host a training camp brought up issues that would remain contentious in cities across the state during the war: prostitution and alcohol. After publicly announcing the locations of the thirty-two training camps, the War Department suddenly withdrew its recommendations until an investigation into vice and prostitution within each of the selected cities had been completed. In San Antonio, local officials found out that more than just a training camp was at stake as military authorities announced that if the city did not clean up its streets, Fort Sam Houston might be closed and the Officers' Training Camp at nearby Camp Funston would be moved. With the army cracking down on prostitution and alcohol, city officials quickly realized they needed to take action to ensure that the city's military installations were not jeopardized. The city engaged in what one historian called a "whirlwind" effort to clean up the city. In fact, in one night, more than one hundred "resorts" in the city were shut down. Fortunately, their effort to clean up the city satisfied the War Department, and it approved San Antonio as the location to train Texas and Oklahoma draftees.[10]

The site selected was adjacent to Fort Sam Houston. Originally named Camp Wilson, it served as a mobilization point for the National Guard in 1916. Re-named in honor of Texas patriot William B. Travis, construction on the camp began on June 14, 1917. Camp Travis covered more than 5,700 acres and cost more than $8 million. By mid-August, nearly 9,000 white and Hispanic laborers were working ten hours per day to build the camp, seven days a week. However, during the construction, four Hispanic members of the Industrial Workers of the World (IWW) were arrested for trying to convince Hispanic workers to stop working unless they were "very well paid." Those arrests and the arrival of troops at the camp discouraged further efforts at unionizing the camp workers. The camp was formally established on July 18, 1917. The first officers and troops began to arrive in mid-August, although the majority of the Texas and Oklahoma draftees arrived in mid-September. In fact, a steady stream of draftees arrived at Camp Travis throughout the war, with the last group passing through the gates in December 1918. In total, approximately 93,792 drafted Texans spent time at Camp Travis alongside approximately 19,816 Oklahoma draftees and thousands more from other states. During November 1917, the camp was home to more than 33,000 soldiers and its population peaked at 35,000 in May 1918. Seven different divisions and non-divisional units passed through Camp Travis during the war. After the armistice, Camp Travis also functioned as a demobilization center, and more than 62,000 soldiers passed through the camp on their way home.[11]

In addition to Camp Travis, the Leon Springs area northwest of San Antonio also played an important role in the area's military development. The U.S. Army established Camp Bullis on September 17, 1917, as a training area. While Camp Bullis contained a cavalry camp, target range, and maneuver range, the army developed the adjacent Camp Leon Springs as an infantry training area and held the first series of the Officers' Training Camps (OTC) there. This initial OTC took place from May 15 to August 11, 1917, and was followed by a second Officers' Training Camp from August 27 to November 27, 1917. Two additional Officers' Training Camps were held in 1918 before the armistice took effect. The Leon Springs area was also home to Camp Stanley, which had been the original military camp in the area, the land having been purchased in 1906 and 1907. In October 1917, the army changed Camp Stanley's name to Camp Funston in honor of former Southern Department Commander General Frederick Funston. The army used Camp Funston for cavalry and artillery training and hosted one of the third series of Officers' Training Camps from January 5 to April 19, 1918. The total area of the target and maneuver ranges encompassed 32,701 acres, of which the government owned 17,274 acres outright and leased another 15,427 acres. One indicator of the army's commitment to the area was the $1.3 million spent on facilities.[12]

The U.S. Army's fledgling Air Service also became heavily involved in San Antonio. While military aviation operations under Captain Benjamin D. Foulois had taken place at Fort Sam Houston as early as 1911, little flying had been done in San Antonio since then. But with the onset of war the Army Air Service expanded its presence in Texas because of the open spaces and excellent flying weather. In the fall of 1916, Foulois returned to San Antonio with orders to find a suitable location for a new flying field. He quickly settled on seven hundred acres southwest of San Antonio with rail access, a water source, and flat ground. After a lease was secured in January 1917, members of the Third Aero Squadron were recruited in San Antonio and began to clear the new field in March. On April 5, 1917, one day before the United States declared war on Germany, four pilots flew from Fort Sam Houston to what would soon come to be known as Kelly Field, named after Lieutenant George E. W. Kelly, who had been killed in a plane crash at Fort Sam Houston in 1911. Kelly Field expanded rapidly as a training base for pilots, instructors, ground officers, mechanics, and bakers and cooks, among others. Its aviation mechanics school had a capacity of 1,300 students, and adjutants, supply officers, and engineers also trained there before departing for places like the Massachusetts Institute of Technology and Ohio State University. It also served as the principal camp for organizing new aviation units for wartime service. Originally divided into Kelly Field number 1 and 2, the government spent more than $6.7 million on improvements to both airfields during the war. Kelly Field 1 eventually encompassed 2,355 acres while Kelly Field Number 2, located adjacent to the original site, sprawled across 1,381 acres. The Air Service also utilized locations within San Antonio itself, where its General Supply Depot was originally located at 114 West Commerce, with branch warehouses at 1903 South Flores Street. In the summer of 1918, those two offices moved to Kelly Field proper, but the Signal Corps kept a General Supply Depot at the intersection of Hays and Cherry Streets. The Air Service's expansion into Texas and San Antonio did not stop with Kelly Field, however.[13]

The second major aviation installation in San Antonio to support World War I training efforts was a former Kelly Field auxiliary landing strip named after Cadet Sydney J. Brooks, who died in a training crash on November 13, 1917. Construction to make the field permanent began on December 11, 1917. Facilities construction and the purchase of additional land at Brooks Field during the war cost more than $1.4 million. The Air Service trained instructor pilots at Brooks Fields, and in the immediate aftermath of the war it served as a balloon school. Brooks Field and later Brooks Air Force Base would remain open until 2006.[14]

Balloon training sites were a unique feature of the World War I aviation landscape, and San Antonio boasted Camp John Wise, located about four miles north of the city. While initially built as a temporary aviation camp, after $250,000 in improvements it became a balloon training site with a capacity of 1,500 students. Both officer and enlisted members of balloon observation companies trained there.[15]

In 1918, near the end of the war, the army established Camp Normoyle in San Antonio as a supply storage area and for motor vehicle maintenance. Only a fraction of the size (88 acres) of nearby Kelly Field, Camp Normoyle facilities construction cost the army approximately $1.7 million. Simply put, the importance of the San Antonio area to the army was immense. The War Department spent more than $19 million on military facilities around the San Antonio area during World War I.[16]

Fort Worth also benefited from a large military presence. Camp Bowie emerged as one of the most significant military sites in the state, and the city became a major hub of aviation training during World War I because of its three flying fields. In May 1917, after the War Department announced that several training camps would be built in the Southern Department, Fort Worth officials put forth a major effort to secure a camp after concluding that it would provide significant economic benefits to the local community. The mayor and other leading citizens wrote a proposal that cited the city's "superb rail facilities" and its status of having the "best horse and mule market" in the state. When General Parker sent several officers to look more closely at Fort Worth, they were shown an area known as Arlington Heights. Shortly thereafter, on June 11, 1917, the army selected Fort Worth as a site for one of the camps and officially established Camp Bowie on July 18, 1917, the same day as Camp Travis. Perhaps unaware of the rivalry between Fort Worth and the large city to its east, the War Department gave the construction contract to a Dallas company, which began work on July 25, 1917.[17]

Although some senior officers and their staffs arrived at Camp Bowie in August and most of the division's soldiers began moving into the camp in early September, construction of the camp was not completed until October. When the Thirty-Sixth Division departed for France in July 1918, Camp Bowie consisted of nearly 3,000 buildings spread across 1,400 acres. Camp Bowie was not the only training facility in the Fort Worth area: A trench system in the Fort Worth suburb of Benbrook took up another 125 acres, while the camp's firing range occupied 756 acres. The total cost of Camp Bowie, including the construction in Benbrook, reached $3.7 million.[18]

In September, Camp Bowie hosted approximately 17,000 National Guardsmen from Texas and Oklahoma. And while the camps had originally been designed to hold either National Guardsmen or draftees, that distinction between the camps soon went away and men were sent where they were needed. For example, Camp Bowie welcomed its first contingent of draftees in October 1917 and like other camps saw a steady stream of them until December 1918. While more than 6,000 Texas draftees trained at Camp Bowie, 16,000 additional draftees came from Oklahoma, Arkansas, California, Louisiana, Iowa, Minnesota, and other states. They even came from the Panama Canal Zone. At its busiest, Camp Bowie supported 41,879 soldiers. After the departure of the Thirty-Sixth Division, Camp Bowie trained infantry replacements and in December 1918, like several other camps, transitioned into a demobilization center. Just prior to the return of the Thirty-Sixth Division in May 1919, the War Department ordered the camp to be salvaged, and it officially closed on August 15, 1919, just over two years after construction had begun. While open, soldiers from eight divisions trained there. Today, Fort Worth's Camp Bowie Boulevard marks the main road that went through the middle of the camp. Outside of a small memorial area, there is little left to indicate that a thriving military base existed there a century ago.[19]

The U.S. Army also established three flying fields near Fort Worth. First came Taliaferro Field in Hicks, about twelve miles northwest of Fort Worth. Construction began on August 31, 1917, but flight operations did not begin until November 20, 1917. Soon after the start of construction on Taliaferro, the army began work on two additional auxiliary airfields in the area that were to be known as Taliaferro 2 and 3. They eventually became separate airfields distinct from Taliaferro. One, Barron Field, located in Everman, six miles south of Fort Worth, was named for Cadet Robert J. Barron, who was killed attempting to rescue the pilots of a crashed airplane in August 1917. Construction began in September 1917, and flying operations began in November. Spread across 600 acres and costing just under $1 million, Barron Field operated an eight-week primary flight school with a capacity of 300 students. The other new airfield was Carruthers Field near Benbrook. Following the same pattern as Barron Field, flying operations at Carruthers Field began in November with an eight-week primary flight school and a course in pursuit aviation. Approximately the same size as Barron, Carruthers cost the army $811,000 to build. The headquarters for all flight training was in Fort Worth, and on May 1, 1918, each field received independent status.[20]

Flight training in Fort Worth was also distinguished by the fact that Canada's Royal Flying Corps (RFC) carried out its training program there. The RFC had already trained U.S. pilots in Canada and operated training fields in New York. However, because of the good flying weather, the RFC expanded its training program into Texas in November 1917, when the Canadian Division of the RFC, under the command of Brigadier General C. G. Hoare, moved its headquarters from Toronto to Fort Worth. RFC training took place at all three fields, and in addition to training their own cadets the RFC continued training American airmen in Fort Worth until March 1918. The RFC training produced ten U.S. squadrons that eventually served on the Western Front.[21]

Dallas also benefited from the military buildup in Texas when the War Department established Love Field and an aviation repair depot in the city. Love Field began as a temporary field, named after Lieutenant Moss Lee Love, who was killed in an aircraft accident in 1913. Construction began in early September 1917, and flying operations commenced in early December. Love Field hosted a bombardment school and served as a temporary camp for reserve pilots. Covering more than 700 acres, the base cost $1.2 million. While the repair depot began as a separate organization from Love Field, on March 21, 1918, the U.S. Army combined the two. Built at a cost of $700,000, the depot's main function was to overhaul and repair aircraft from fields across Texas. Finally, the army established a temporary camp on the site of the state fairgrounds. Known as Camp Dick for Cadet James F. Dick, who was killed in an accident in Dallas on January 6, 1918, the camp served as a place to consolidate graduates of the various ground schools until they began their flight training. By the time the war ended, more than 25,000 pilots had spent time at Camp Dick, which caused it to be celebrated as the largest aviation camp in the United States. Thousands of men passed through the camp as they transitioned from one base to another for training. As the *New York Times* put it, at Camp Dick the "men were able to keep up their studies in a military atmosphere during periods when they could not be cared for at the schools."[22]

Besides hosting Camp Dick, the state fairgrounds also supported the war effort by displaying British war equipment during the 1917 Texas State Fair. Described as the "greatest display of its kind" the exhibit consisted of numerous weapons and tools used on the Western Front, including long-range cannons, submarine torpedoes, howitzers, gas masks, trench periscopes, machine guns, and "scores of other death-dealing weapons that are snuffing out the lives of soldiers across the sea," as one paper reported. Overall, the exhibit contained more than twenty-five tons of equipment and was billed as "one of the chief attractions of the State Fair." The Red Cross Society received the funds generated from ticket sales.[23]

Houston was not left out of the burst of military construction associated with the war. The War Department built two major military installations there: Camp Logan and Ellington Field. Camp Logan, named after Mexican War and Civil War veteran John A. Logan, was, like Camp Bowie and Camp Travis, formally established on July 18, 1917. Construction began a week later and continued throughout 1918. Camp Logan hosted approximately 20,000 members of the Illinois National Guard's Thirty-Third Division, which occupied the camp until May 1918. Under the command of Major General George Bell Jr., the Thirty-Third Division became the second National Guard division that trained in the state to depart for the Western Front on April 23, 1918, behind the Thirty-Second Division, which trained at Waco. After the departure of the Thirty-Third Division, more than 32,000 draftees trained at the camp before the November 1918 armistice. After a stint as a demobilization center after the war, Camp Logan closed on March 20, 1919, and was turned over to the U.S. Public Health Service. Camp Logan had a capacity of 44,899 soldiers, covered a total of 9,560 acres, and cost approximately $4 million. At its peak in December 1917, 33,346 soldiers called the camp home, although its strength slowly decreased from that point until the armistice. Elements of six different divisions passed through Camp Logan during the war. As noted previously, Camp Logan was also the scene of the Houston Riots in the late summer of 1917, which exposed long-simmering racial tension in Houston.[24]

The U.S. Army built Ellington Field southeast of Houston and named it after Second Lieutenant Eric L. Ellington, a cavalry officer killed in an aviation accident in 1913. Like other Texas airfields, construction began in September and flying operations began in early December 1917. The field hosted an armorer's school briefly in 1918, but Ellington's primary focus was on its 600 student bombing school. Farther southeast, in San Leon, on the shores of Galveston Bay, the army operated an aerial gunnery school for graduates of the bombing school. While the 1,815 acres for Ellington Field cost $126,000, the army spent more than $2.3 million on facilities there. The army also established a temporary aviation general supply depot at City Wharf No. 4, six miles from Houston, in June 1918. It was used as a warehouse and extra storage space for additional aircraft, parts, and engines from Ellington. At its largest, the aviation general supply depot offered 380,000 square feet of storage space and remained open through 1919. To this day, Ellington Field remains an active air base for the Texas Air National Guard.[25]

The army also established a temporary flying field at Park Place in Harris County. Known as Ream Field, after a brief construction period in the summer of 1918 the field functioned for a short period, from September 23, 1918, through October 5, 1918, under the control of the 2nd Provisional Wing. The Air Service abandoned Ream Field on March 4, 1919.[26]

Waco also benefited from the military buildup in the state. Like San Antonio, Houston, and Fort Worth, Waco was selected to host one of the army's thirty-two training camps. After Waco's selection, one local paper crowed that "Waco will be known all over the world as the location of a great army cantonment and a colossal aviation camp." Located on high ground just one-half mile from the city, Camp MacArthur was named for General Arthur MacArthur Jr., the father of future General of the Army Douglas MacArthur. Construction began on July 20, 1917, and on September 12, 1917, the camp officially opened and welcomed thousands of National Guardsmen from Michigan and Wisconsin to begin their training as part of the Thirty-Second "Red Arrow" Division under the command of Major General James Parker, who had recently commanded the Southern Department. Camp MacArthur's 1,377 acres could hold up to 45,000 soldiers, although the number of men training there never exceeded 28,000. Less than a month after the 18,000 National Guardsmen from Michigan and Wisconsin arrived, the camp received its first complement of draftees, which included men from Arkansas, Missouri, New Mexico, Texas, Wisconsin, and several other states. Excess troops from Kelly Field in San Antonio, which had become too congested, were also housed at Camp MacArthur. As it turned out, the Thirty-Second Division was the first of the divisions that trained in Texas to depart for the Western Front, leaving Waco in January 1918. In fact, the Red Arrow Division left so quickly that it was short 3,500 men. Still, when the flow of draftees ended in November 1918, more than 51,000 had passed through Camp MacArthur's gates, and when the armistice went into effect, 21,000 men were still training there. Construction of Camp MacArthur was estimated at $5 million. After the departure of the Red Arrow Division in January 1918, Camp MacArthur trained replacements, hosted one of the fourth series of Officers'

Training Schools from September to December 1918, and functioned as a demobilization facility, where it processed 11,000 men for discharge after the war. Salvaging of the camp began in January 1919, and much of the material was earmarked for use in building border stations. Camp MacArthur officially closed on March 7, 1919.[27] Rich Field was built adjacent to Camp MacArthur beginning in September 1917 and opened for flying operations in early December, at a construction cost of more than $1.1 million.[28]

While San Antonio, Fort Worth, Dallas, Houston, and Waco had the most significant influx of military infrastructure projects in the state, several other cities also benefited from the military expansion. In Wichita Falls, for example, the U.S. Army established Call Field in honor of Lieutenant Loren H. Call, who was killed in 1913. Built at a cost of just over $1.1 million, flying operations there began in December 1917. Call Field hosted a three hundred-student observation school and served as a reserve military aviators' concentration area like Dallas's Love Field. Surprisingly, El Paso failed to secure a new military training facility, in part because Secretary of War Baker expressed concern about prostitution and vice there. Although city officials worked hard to clean up their city, the facility was never built.[29] The Texas National Guard operated a semi-permanent camp in Corpus Christi, known as Camp Scurry. The U.S. Army operated General Hospital No. 15 in the same city beginning in January 1918. Located in the Corpus Beach Hotel and Bathing Pavilion, the facility was used primarily as a convalescent hospital until it was transferred to the Public Health Service on May 31, 1919. The army also established a temporary flying field near Sanderson in remote Terrell County to aid in patrolling the Big Bend region.[30]

While the U.S. Army had a long-established presence in Texas dating back to the mid-nineteenth century, the U.S. intervention in World War I resulted in a phenomenal increase in military facilities across the state. This brought the war home to Texans who would never come close to the fighting on the Western Front. In addition, it set a precedent for the remainder of the century in which Texas hosted significant numbers of military personnel of the U.S. Army, Air Force, and Navy, as well as supported a growing defense industry. The military presence in Texas during World War I established a pattern that would continue during World War II and beyond.[31]

As the summer of 1917 slipped away, a flurry of frenzied activity across the country and in Texas began to wind down. While many thousands of Texans were just starting training, others were already on their way to France to serve with General Pershing's American Expeditionary Forces. Among the first Texas soldiers to leave for France were four companies of soldiers from Dallas, Houston, Ogden, and Big Spring, which departed Fort Worth for France as part of the 117th Supply Train under the command of Major William Devine. The 117th served with the famed Forty-Second, or "Rainbow" Division, so called because the division included units from many different states.[32]

The War Department had created the AEF to execute military operations on the Western Front under the command of General Pershing. In the United States, the responsibility for organizing, training, and equipping the AEF fell to the army chief of staff, General Tasker H. Bliss and later General Peyton C. March. The deployment of such a large military force overseas presented problems with command and control that took much trial and error before a workable system of cooperation and command between General Pershing's AEF in Europe and the War Department in Washington had matured. While work was in progress to raise the required numbers of soldiers for the war, army leaders had learned much from the conduct of the war in Europe and had concluded that the army's organizational structure had to be changed to accommodate the trench warfare common to the Western Front. This new organizational structure took effect in August 1917, just as hundreds of thousands of soldiers were arriving at their training camps. Essentially, the U.S. Army organized its divisions into three components: Regular Army, National Guard, and National Army (draftees). Divisions numbered from one to twenty-five represented Regular Army divisions. All National Guard divisions carried designations between twenty-six and seventy-five, and National Army divisions used designations seventy-six and higher. Using such designations, of course, resulted in an implicit assumption that lower numbered divisions contained more experienced, professional soldiers, while higher numbered divisions indicated less experienced draftees who might have morale problems. As it turned out, over the course of the war, with transfers and replacements, most of the divisions could not be defined so easily and such early assumptions no longer held true by war's end. Based on the army's new organizational structure, the Texas and Oklahoma National Guard troops consolidating at Camp Bowie in Fort Worth became the Thirty-Sixth Division, while the Texas and Oklahoma draftees who were assigned to Camp Travis in San Antonio became the Ninetieth Division.[33]

The two "Texas" divisions trained at Camp Bowie and Camp Travis from September 1917 until June 1918. Major General Edwin St. John Greble commanded the Thirty-Sixth Division at Camp Bowie. By all accounts, Greble was an effective leader, although his age would hamper his progression in the wartime army. In 1917, he turned fifty-nine years old, which concerned General Pershing, who generally preferred younger officers for the rigors of divisional command on the Western Front. In order to weed out unfit generals, Pershing brought a large group of them to France in the fall of 1917, ostensibly to tour the Western Front but actually for Pershing to gauge their fitness for command. At the end of the visit, Pershing determined that General Greble would not be able to physically withstand the rigors of combat. While he continued to train the Thirty-Sixth Division at Camp Bowie, he would not lead it to France.[34]

In the summer of 1918, just as the Thirty-Sixth Division prepared to embark for France, Pershing removed General Greble from divisional command and replaced him with Major General William R. Smith. At the time he received word of his promotion to division command, Smith commanded the Sixty-Second Field Artillery Brigade of the Thirty-Seventh Division at Camp Sheridan in Montgomery, Alabama. Smith did not join the division at Camp Bowie but rather met the division on July 6, 1918, as it prepared to sail from New Jersey. In fact, Smith was already in New York preparing to embark with the Sixty-Second Field Artillery when he received his orders to the Thirty-Sixth Division. A West Point graduate and ten years younger than Greble, Smith was a farsighted choice to the lead the former National Guardsmen. He not only would command them during their entire time in France, but would also bring them back to Texas and Oklahoma after the war ended.[35]

The Ninetieth Division trained at San Antonio's Camp Travis under the leadership of Major General Henry T. Allen. Like Greble, Allen was a Regular Army officer. A native of Kentucky, General Allen graduated from West Point in 1882 and joined the cavalry.

After an extensive career that included service in the Spanish-American War and the Philippines, Allen served with Pershing during the latter's expedition into Mexico in pursuit of Pancho Villa. In May 1917, the army promoted him to brigadier general and on August 5, the same day that President Wilson federalized the National Guard, he received his second star. Slightly more than two weeks later, on August 25th, he assumed command of Camp Travis and began the task of organizing the first contingents of Texas and Oklahoma draftees. Like Greble, General Allen visited the Western Front in November 1917 for closer scrutiny by Pershing.[36] Although only one year younger than Greble, Pershing believed Allen had the necessary physical stamina to succeed on the Western Front. As the *San Antonio Express* observed, at fifty-eight years old General Allen was "one of the best-preserved men in the army, not appearing to be more than 45 years old." The paper also stated that he was "a man of charming personality" and was a "great leader of men, possessing the confidence and admiration from all those associated with him, both as fellow officers and enlisted men." General Allen would lead the Ninetieth through its training and into battle on the Western Front through the armistice.[37]

While the organizational and bureaucratic changes related to organizing an army of millions were being implemented in September 1917, the thousands of men at training camps and airfields across the nation began their training. Upon arrival at camp, the new soldiers received physicals and shots, their first uniforms, learned to set up tents, did calisthenics and drill, went on long hikes to improve their conditioning, and began to learn about the weapons they would use at the front. Combat training included time in specially designed trench complexes where the new soldiers lived upwards of forty-eight hours at a time to get a feel for trench warfare. They went to firing ranges and spent more time than they ever imagined training for gas warfare and standing guard duty. Besides the physical aspects of training, instructors introduced them to the Articles of War, the "obligations and rights of the soldier," whistle and arm signals, and first aid. The army also hired instructors from local universities to teach rudimentary French, math, and bookkeeping, among myriad other subjects. They spent countless hours in the classroom and the drill field. Interestingly, officers soon found out that many of their "Doughboys" could not read or write.

To help rectify that, officers paired illiterate soldiers with comrades who could.[38]

In the summer of 1917, the army also began a series of Officers Training Camps aimed at producing thousands of new officers for the wartime army. Each camp lasted approximately ninety days and graduates earned the somewhat sarcastic sobriquet "90-day wonders." Thousands of men applied for a chance to earn a commission in the army. The first series of camps were held at thirteen locations, which included Leon Springs; the second series at nine locations; and the third series, from January to April 1918, took place at twenty-seven locations around the country. This third series was sponsored by the National Army divisions, and the Ninetieth held its own OTC at Camp Travis, which graduated five Texans and Oklahomans who had been enlisted members of the division. However, because the division did not have a need for that many officers, the graduates returned to their units as sergeants until officer positions became available.[39]

While the army trained its ground forces at the four camps in the state, training of Air Service cadets proved to be challenging and dangerous because of the volume of flight activity. This was amply illustrated by one day at San Antonio's Kelly Field, where officers and cadets set a record by flying 135 aircraft for a total of 882 flight hours. With air training, there were bound to be accidents, from the most seasoned flyers to cadets on their first solo flight. In one case, General C. G. Hoare, the commander of the British Royal Flying Corps in Canada and the United States, crashed at Taliaferro Field outside of Fort Worth in March 1918 and was severely injured. While training deaths were common, the death of the world-famous dancer Vernon Castle at Carruthers Field shook the flying community to the core. As the *New York Times* reported, "All Fort Worth, Camp Bowie, and the aviation fields plainly showed the deepest regret at his death." By the end of February 1918, forty-seven fliers had been killed in Texas, and thirty-three of those had occurred at the Fort Worth airfields. Many were British, and the large numbers of deaths among that group was attributed to their "more strenuous system of practice and drill." To put it simply, learning to fly in Texas during World War I was so dangerous that in May 1918, the *New York Times* ran an article that noted the deaths of seven American flyers. Four had been killed in France and three in Texas.

Flight training in Texas could be almost as dangerous as aerial combat on the Western Front.[40]

As training progressed through the fall of 1917 and as the weather began to turn, the close quarters of thousands of men in the training camps proved to be a breeding ground for sickness and disease. The sudden and rapid rise in sickness among men who had not been exposed to many ailments while growing up in rural towns required swift action on the part of the War Department to ensure that diseases did not turn into epidemics in both the military and civilian populations. Still, pneumonia and influenza took an enormous toll on soldiers and civilians during the war. In its efforts to prevent disease and illness from hampering training, the Wilson administration followed a similar approach to that taken to prevent vice around the training camps by ensuring attention was given to proper sanitation practices and the prevention of disease. Working with state and local governments, the War Department focused on stemming the tide of infectious diseases. But as more and more soldiers were taken ill and died, Major General William C. Gorgas, the surgeon general of the army, visited four training camps across the country to assess their sanitary conditions in the fall and winter of 1917. During his visit to Camp Bowie in December 1917, the magnitude of the problem became clear. The camp hospital had a capacity of 1,000 but held 1,867 patients. After meeting with Governor Hobby, Gorgas sent his report to Army Chief of Staff General Tasker H. Bliss. He noted that in November 1917 Camp Bowie had more than 3,000 cases of pneumonia and measles that had caused the deaths of forty-one soldiers. He also stated that Camp Bowie had the worst sanitary conditions of the four camps he visited.[41]

Many officials attributed the sickness in the camps to a lack of winter clothing, and General Greble wrote several letters to the War Department stressing the need for proper clothing to avert sickness. Unfortunately, relief was slow in coming because the War Department had never needed to clothe and equip so many soldiers in such a short time. Many of Greble's soldiers did not receive overcoats until just before Christmas. Still, testifying before Congress on the issue of sickness and the lack of clothing and equipment, when asked if the epidemic could have been prevented if the camp had better sewage and plenty of clothing, General Greble stated, "I do not say the epidemic could have been prevented, but certainly many lives would have been saved."[42]

Fortunately, the efforts by the army to improve sanitary and living conditions in the camps paid dividends, particularly for Camp Bowie, which received an influx of doctors and nurses, hot baths, and a new sewer system. In addition, General Gorgas wanted more tents, so the camp could house fewer soldiers per tent to help stop the spread of germs. Illustrative of the fears of foreign sabotage that were prevalent at the time, General Gorgas also adamantly dismissed any notion that German "intrigues" had been responsible for the pneumonia epidemic across the southern camps. As the winter of 1917–18 gave way to the spring, conditions at the camps across the country slowly improved, although pneumonia remained a problem at San Antonio's Camp Travis and measles continued to affect all four Texas camps. On Christmas Day, 1,200 soldiers remained hospitalized at Camp Bowie. And as 1917 came to an end, a single War Department statistic told the grim tale of sickness in the stateside training camps. Since July 1917, the AEF in France had lost 317 soldiers. Over that same period in the United States, 2,918 soldiers had succumbed to sickness or accidents in training camps.[43]

After the new year, training picked up again. More drill, marksmanship, trench warfare, and myriad other programs and courses continued without let up. While brand new recruits may have benefited from the training, the men who had been in the camps since the previous September had begun to champ at the bit, wondering when they would go overseas, and the *Dallas Morning News* reported that "something that resembles a spirit of unrest now prevails in some of the units."[44]

In order the keep their men focused, the two "Texas" divisions held major parades in Fort Worth and San Antonio that seemed to indicate the two divisions were ready for the Western Front. Camp Bowie soldiers from the Thirty-Sixth Division paraded through Forth Worth in November 1917 in front of an estimated 30,000 people. Governor Hobby, who was in Fort Worth at the time and watched the parade, stressed how those current soldiers represented the state's past: "When I see the proud stride and flashing eyes of these young soldiers I am reminded of the heroes of San

Jacinto," he was reported to have said. If the November parade was impressive, the Thirty-Sixth Division review held in February 1918 was even more so. Described as "a parting gift to the people of Texas and Oklahoma," an estimated 150,000 to 225,000 watched nearly 25,000 soldiers, 5,000 animals, and at least 1,200 vehicles of the division on a three-hour parade through the city. Likewise, the Ninetieth Division at Camp Travis held several reviews in San Antonio, with former President William Howard Taft, Postmaster General Albert S. Burleson, and Governor Hobby among the many distinguished visitors in attendance. The Ninetieth Division paraded through San Antonio in February 1918, in honor of George Washington's birthday. An estimated 100,000 people watched 20,000 soldiers parade toward the reviewing stand in Alamo Plaza.[45]

Then, on June 5, 1918, General Allen's Ninetieth Division received orders for France. Ten days later, the division was at Camp Mills, New York, and the divisional headquarters departed for France on June 21, 1918, aboard the USS *Shropshire*. About the time that the Ninetieth Division arrived in France, the Thirty-Sixth Division at Camp Bowie finally received its orders to depart on July 2, 1918. As the soldiers boarded trains that would take them east, where transports awaited them that would take them to their destiny as soldiers in the AEF, General Greble could only watch.[46]

The summer of 1918 was a busy time for the army as thousands of soldiers completed their training at camps across the country and began streaming toward the East Coast along rail lines all over the country.[47] There, the soldiers boarded waiting transports for the two-week trip across the Atlantic. The pace of movement had increased significantly as the AEF had begun to bolster its presence on the Western Front and the fresh-faced "Soldier Boys" and "Doughboys" began arriving in France in significant numbers. The thousands of Texans who served in the AEF joined the millions of soldiers from other nations who occupied the trenches of the Western Front. It had been a long road for many of these Texans, starting in the summer of 1917 or even earlier. They had seen their communities and state rally around the Wilson administration, they had seen the fear many of their fellow citizens experienced regarding espionage and sabotage, they had seen how their communities had found ways to participate in what many perceived as a great struggle to preserve democracy in the world, and they had seen how their fellow citizens supported them as they joined the military and trained at locations across Texas. Now, those Texans were "Over There" preparing to join the fighting in one of the most destructive wars the world had ever seen.[48]

*Chapter 6*

# TEXANS IN COMBAT

Although the United States was officially at war on April 6, 1917, months passed before American soldiers began arriving in France, and the majority did not do so until the spring and summer of 1918. Their arrival came at a critical moment of the war. In March 1918, the German army had launched a massive offensive, known as Operation Michael, along the Western Front as it attempted to break the armies of Great Britain and France before the Americans could tip the scales in the Allies' favor. While the German offensive made initial progress, by summer the campaign had bogged down, and it became increasingly clear that the offensive would not meet its strategic goal. As the German offensive stalled, thousands upon thousands of American soldiers were funneled onto the Western Front. American troops participated in several major battles that summer, including Cantigny and Belleau Wood, where they won respect and legendary status as the "Rock of the Marne." While the Americans began to prove their mettle in battle, thousands more arrived every day in European ports such as Brest, Saint-Nazaire, and Liverpool. From there, they moved to training camps deep within the French countryside only one hundred miles from the front.

From the moment he assumed command of the American Expeditionary Force (AEF), General John J. Pershing struggled with the Allied leadership over the best way to use American troops on the Western Front. The Allied leadership argued that American forces should be assimilated into British and French divisions already at the front. Pershing, on the other hand, wanted an independent American army to fight alongside the British and French. The "amalgamation controversy" remained a contentious issue during the American build-up in France. In the end Pershing got his way with the establishment of the American First Army. American troops would not be assimilated into British and French units. As a compromise, Pershing did loan several complete American divisions to the British and French, and in the summer of 1918 Pershing assigned the American II Corps to the British army, where it trained under British supervision and even traded its U.S. equipment for British equivalents. In the fall of 1918, Pershing also assigned several U.S. divisions to the French, one of which was the Thirty-Sixth Division with its large contingent of Texas and Oklahoma National Guardsmen. The Ninetieth Division, however, with its Texas and Oklahoma draftees, joined the American First Army and soon saw extensive fighting.

The U.S. troops who had been in France since the earliest days of the American intervention included plenty of Texans who were not part of the Thirty-Sixth and Ninetieth Divisions. By June 1918, the AEF had already suffered more than 10,000 killed and wounded in fighting on the Western Front, including Fredericksburg native Louis J. Jordan, who was killed in March 1918 while serving with the Forty-Second Division. Jordan was the first Texas officer killed in the war. Another Texas officer, Captain George F. Wellage of Eagle Pass, received coverage in the *New York Times* because he "smoked out a machine gun nest, killed a German officer in combat, and then captured a second officer whom he had wounded." Indeed, newspapers had long been reporting on wounded Texas servicemen who were returning to the United States for convalescence, such as Lufkin's Hubert Hill, who suffered from mustard gas and could only speak in whispers, and Private Charles G. Hopkins of Madisonville, who claimed to be the "first American wounded in action." Whether true or not—and Hopkins's claim is doubtful—the return of men who had already been wounded before the National Guardsmen and draftees had even left the state must have compounded their frustration prior to shipping out for France.[1]

For most of the Texans who crossed the Atlantic with the Thirty-Sixth or Ninetieth Divisions, the trip across involved nothing more serious that seasickness, although German submarines were a constant threat. Upon arriving in France, one soldier wrote simply, "We were twelve days crossing the fish pond . . . I was sure glad to see dirt again." For many Texans, their first glimpses of life in a foreign country proved instructive. The Texans marveled at the sight of German prisoners of war who were working on the French docks. One North Texas soldier wrote to his father, "I like this country fine, but it is queer; the buildings are strange looking structures, and the people wear wooden shoes." Another Texan, from Wichita Falls, wrote that France was "a beautiful country, everything looks different from the part of the U.S.A. I started from," while a Wise County soldier wrote to his mother that "we are in an ancient city and there are lots of wonderful things to see and there are lots of things that are amusing to a boy who never travelled much." General Pershing, as was his habit, inspected newly arrived units in the Ninetieth and Thirty-Sixth Divisions. He later recalled in his memoirs that the Texans and Oklahomans were impatient when told they could not be moved immediately to the front but had more training to complete.[2]

In mid-August 1918, after more than a year of training, the Ninetieth Division began the final steps of its journey to the Western Front, where they would eventually serve seventy-five days in combat in both of the U.S. Army's major offensives, at Saint-Mihiel and the Meuse-Argonne. Assigned to the U.S. First Army and following the normal practice of the AEF, the Ninetieth Division moved into a quiet sector of the front behind the First Division. Prior to going into the lines, General Allen sent a telegram to Texas Governor Hobby to mark the troops' departure:

> This is just a word to tell you that the 90th Division has successfully completed its final training and is now about to move to the front. The division is in excellent health and fine spirits. The complimentary reports made on it by training experts reflect credit on Texas and Oklahoma . . . The appearance of the men marked vitality and fighting force. They will be a genuine asset in the coming months over here, but a still greater one to their states when they return, by reason of the broad increment of their education.[3]

After a week in reserve, General Allen's division received orders to relieve the 1st Division in the Villers-en-Haye sector, between the Eighty-Second and Eighty-Ninth U.S. Divisions on August 24,

1918, about the time the Thirty-Sixth Division had settled into its training program behind the lines.[4]

From August 24 until the start of the Saint-Mihiel offensive on September 12, the Ninetieth Division conducted local operations along a nine-kilometer front in the Villers-en-Haye sector. The division's 180th "Texas" Brigade occupied the eastern portion of the lines while the 179th "Oklahoma" brigade held positions to the west. One officer from San Antonio, Lieutenant J. Montgomery Fly, described his brigade's movement "up to the firing line," in what would be his last letter home before being killed in combat. During the next several weeks, the division carried out patrols and gained experience in trench warfare. During this period, the division suffered its first combat casualties, losing ten men killed, thirty-nine wounded, and one missing. Things were about to change for the division, as AEF planners selected the division to participate in the first major offensive of the U.S. First Army.[5]

The Allied powers had planned a major offensive to take place in the fall of 1918, with the French pushing the German army back across the Aisne River, the British pushing toward Cambrai, and the Americans aiming for Sedan. However, General Pershing had already planned for a smaller operation to be carried out by the First Army to reduce a German salient in the front lines near Saint-Mihiel. This operation marked the debut in battle of the First Army. Planners hoped that the offensive would open several highways and threaten German positions near the town of Metz. However, with the pending Allied offensive, the First Army was forced to scale back its attack on the Saint-Mihiel salient so it could participate in the larger Meuse-Argonne offensive. Because it was already in location along the southern face of the salient, the Ninetieth, along with several other divisions, was slated to participate in this major offensive. As part of General Hunter Liggett's I Corps, the Ninetieth pivoted slightly while the divisions to its left (west) attacked to the northeast. Although the Ninetieth was an untested division, morale was high and even General Pershing noted the division's enthusiasm for the upcoming battle.[6]

On September 12, the Saint-Mihiel offensive began with an artillery barrage in the dark, rainy, and foggy early morning hours. The Ninetieth Division attacked directly north into the Bois de Friere and Bois Saint Claude, with the Eighty-Second Division on the left and the Fifth Division on the right. By the end of the first day, the attacking divisions had reached their initial objectives. The offensive continued over the next three days, and on September 16 the division consolidated its positions as the Saint-Mihiel offensive came to an end. The son of former Governor James S. Hogg, Mike Hogg, who served with the Ninetieth during the battle, wrote afterward, "I am just back from the big American 'push'—St. Mihiel. We were in it up to our eyes. Almost two weeks, we dug, marched, fought and scrambled around in something I know was worse than Hell itself. But here we are, as happy as if we all had good sense—men and all."[7]

While the First Army considered the operation successful, it did not represent a major loss for the German army. The Germans fought aggressively, and the Ninetieth Division suffered for it, with casualties totaling sixty-eight officers and 1,683 men, including eleven officers and 220 enlisted men killed. The division also lost slightly more than 300 horses and mules in the fighting, which were a critically important resource for World War I divisions. Nevertheless, Texans in the divisions fought bravely. Fort Worth native Major Thomas D. Collins famously told his men, "Don't call me major, call me Slim," as he led his men past machine gun fire and barbed wire emplacements. Another officer, Major Mike Ashburn, although wounded, led his men throughout the fighting until a second wound forced his evacuation. Perhaps more importantly, the Ninetieth Division learned some valuable lessons and applied them during the upcoming Meuse-Argonne offensive. The division performed well in the offensive, and as one soldier wrote to his father in San Antonio, "The Ninetieth Division held up their end."[8]

Although the Meuse-Argonne offensive began on September 26, the Ninetieth Division initially played a supporting role. Along with several other supporting divisions, the Ninetieth was tasked with carrying out a diversionary attack, or "demonstration," along the front to confuse the Germans regarding the true location of the offensive. Unfortunately, German intelligence had caught wind of an impending "great attack," and the German troops were ready for the Ninetieth as it attacked on the morning of September 26. Although the demonstration did not result in any major gains, it did help mask the location of the main attack from the Germans. But that was small comfort to the soldiers involved who lost their friends and comrades in the "demonstration." General Allen was dismayed by the losses and wrote his wife, "I will never be able to take back to Texas and Oklahoma as many of their sons as I had hoped."[9]

After the diversionary attack, Allen's division continued to carry out local patrols and raids until October 10, when the U.S. Seventh Division relieved General Allen's soldiers. From the end of the Saint-Mihiel campaign on September 16, until its relief on October 10, the Ninetieth Division suffered approximately 1,830 men killed and wounded. The division moved into First Army Reserve back at Toul, and after several days of rest and recuperation, on October 13, the Ninetieth Division moved to Nixeville, near Verdun, on the same day that the other "Texas" division, the Thirty-Sixth, took up positions along the Aisne River to the west.[10]

After five days near Nixeville, the Ninetieth joined General John Hines's III Corps as a reserve division while the First Army's great Meuse-Argonne offensive continued to rage between the Meuse River and the Argonne Forest. After several days in reserve, the Ninetieth relieved the Fifth Division on October 21. Joining the third phase of the Meuse-Argonne offensive, the division was charged with strengthening the American presence in the Bois de Rappes, capturing the town of Bantheville, and straightening the American lines. Two days later, on October 23, the Ninetieth Division captured Bantheville and Bourrate. Over the next several days, the division battled Germans embedded between the Bois de Rappes and Bois de Bantheville and conducted an exhausting battle to capture a small rise known as Hill 270. After several days of skirmishing and local fighting, the division attacked north on November 1, 1918, and pushed the line forward at a cost of more than 1,400 casualties. For the next five days, through November 6, 1918, the division pressed its attack and finally reached the Meuse River at Sassey-sur-Meuse and Laneuville-sur-Meuse. On the night of November 9–10, the division crossed the Meuse and prepared to attack again on November 11, 1918. However, those attacks were called off, and the division spent the morning of November 11, 1918, strengthening its positions near the town of Baâlon. The Ninetieth's front line positions stretched westward along the high ground northwest of the town and along the eastern edge of Stenay, a few miles to the west along the Meuse. Finally, at 11 a.m. on that day, the armistice went into effect and the Ninetieth Division's time in the crucible of war came to an end, but not before Corporal Carl Sheffield of the 360th Infantry regiment was killed by German artillery fire in Mouzay approximately thirty minutes before the end of fighting.[11]

While several sources provide total casualties for the Ninetieth Division during the war, the American Battle Monuments Commission (AMBC) calculated the number at 7,539, which included 758 killed during Saint-Mihiel and 730 killed during the Meuse-Argonne. The Ninetieth Division spent seventy-five days in the front lines and participated in some of the fiercest fighting in the American sector during the fall of 1918, particularly in the Meuse-Argonne from October 22 until the armistice.[12]

While the Ninetieth Division participated in the fighting as part of the U.S. First Army, the other "Texas" division faced its own trial by fire. The Thirty-Sixth Division arrived in France just as the Ninetieth Division began its move to the front. At the time, General William R. Smith's division consisted of 965 officers and 25,922 enlisted men, many of them Texans. The division moved to its training area near Bar-sur-Aube, having already suffered its first casualty in France when a soldier riding on top of one of the railroad cars was struck by a low overpass and instantly killed. Once at their training area, the division's units were housed in small villages scattered around the area as they began their training program that focused on the AEF's technique of maneuver, or "open" warfare, primarily field exercises that emphasized maneuvering in open terrain rather than in trench warfare. Like the Ninetieth Division, the AEF planned for its divisions such as the Thirty-Sixth to spend one month in the training area, one month in a reserve role behind the front, and a third month in a quiet sector of the line with an experienced division before carrying out offensive combat operations. However, the Thirty-Sixth never had the chance to finish this training program before it was thrown into the fight.[13]

After only one month in its training area, the Thirty-Sixth Division began moving toward the front in late September 1918. Although the division had seen a large influx of new soldiers, a significant number of Texans remained, including some in key leadership positions. Many other Texans had left the division due to transfers and other reasons, including Brigadier General Henry

Hutchings, who had been the state's National Guard adjutant general and had been serving as the Seventy-First Brigade commander. While in the training area, the AEF inspector general believed that Hutchings had shown such a lack of proficiency that he recommended General Smith relieve him of his duties, which Smith did with General Pershing's concurrence on August 29, 1918. The army offered Hutchings a commission as a major and a new assignment, but Hutchings refused and returned to Texas on October 1, 1918, a week before the brigade he had trained at Camp Bowie and led to France went into combat. Brigadier General Pegram Whitworth, who was from the state of Washington, replaced Hutchings and led the Seventy-First Brigade through the remainder of the war. Despite the loss of Hutchings, other prominent Texans remained with the division, including General Hutchings's son, Lieutenant Colonel Edwin Hutchings.[14] General Hulen remained in command of the Seventy-Second Brigade, while Austin attorney Colonel Bloor remained in command of the 142nd Infantry Regiment. Likewise, Lieutenant Colonels Alvin Owsley and William Culberson, who were both relatives of well-known Texans, still served on the divisional staff.[15]

When the Thirty-Sixth and Ninetieth Divisions went into combat, they could no longer be considered Texas and Oklahoma divisions. Still, they did contain a sizable percentage of soldiers from those states and were considered by many Texans at home to be "their" divisions. As an example, when Colonel Alfred Wainwright Bloor's 142nd Infantry went into the line in October 1918, only 46 percent of the original Texas National Guardsmen remained with the unit. The other 54 percent had joined the regiment either at Camp Bowie or while the regiment trained in France. In addition, while many thousands of Texans served in those two divisions, thousands of other Texans continued to serve in other AEF units, such as the Forty-Second "Rainbow" Division, which included a young Brigadier General Douglas MacArthur among its leaders.[16]

While the Ninetieth Division spent most of the last three months of the war at or near the front and participated in both major U.S. Army campaigns, the Thirty-Sixth Division did not receive the call to join the fighting until late September. After a month of training behind the lines, on September 26, 1918, the same day that the Ninetieth carried out its "demonstration," General Smith's Division finally received orders to the front. Instead of joining Pershing's First Army, the Thirty-Sixth Division, along with the Second "Indianhead" Division, received orders to link up with the French Group of Armies of the Center (GAC), where the Thirty-Sixth promptly went into reserve. Soon, the Thirty-Sixth Division joined the French Fourth Army under the command of General Henri Gouraud. Working in conjunction with Pershing's First Army, which would advance east of the Argonne Forest, Gouraud's army would keep pace along the western side of the Argonne. The two armies expected to link up north of the forest and continue the advance side by side.[17]

Soon, General Gouraud ordered the Thirty-Sixth Division to join the fighting in France's devastated Champagne region. First, General Whitworth's Seventy-First Brigade was transferred to the French Twenty-First Army Corps, which in early October was engaged in combat operations near the French towns of Suippes and Somme Suippes. There, units of the Thirty-Sixth division went into combat for the first time. Although initially designated as a reserve unit, the fluid nature of the front forced the French to use the inexperienced brigade to relieve the American Second Division, which had just fought a difficult and bloody battle at Blanc Mont, a small hill south of the village of Saint-Etienne. Using an untested brigade to relieve an entire division was a risky move on the part of the French, but they had little choice. Thus, General Whitworth's two regiments, the 141st and the 142nd, prepared to move into the lines. During the relief, the two regiments were placed under the control of the Second Division commander, U.S. Marine Corps Major General John Lejeune. Lejeune was aware of the inexperience of the former National Guardsmen and argued that they were not ready but to no avail. After the relief, Whitworth's brigade could expect to attack German positions near Saint-Etienne.[18]

On the evening of October 6, the 141st and 142nd Infantry regiments moved toward the front. The march immediately went wrong as the guides got lost, forcing several of the 142nd's companies to wander the front lines during the night looking for their positions. Finally, at 3:00 a.m. Colonel Bloor received the coded message "13 children are in bed," meaning that the regiment's companies had finally reached their frontline positions. Fortunately, the attack contemplated for October 7 was postponed for twenty-four hours, giving the two regiments a brief but welcome respite.

The inexperience of the brigade was soon apparent. Planning for the attack was confused, and units relied on verbal orders rather than written ones because there was simply not enough time. Furthermore, the available maps turned out to be useless. Finally, after several meetings with the brigade and division commanders, the two regimental colonels issued verbal orders to their battalion commanders at approximately 3:00 a.m. on the morning of October 8. In turn, the battalion commanders verbally briefed their company commanders around 5:00 a.m., only fifteen minutes before the proposed attack time. When one company commander noted that it was already 5:10 a.m., he was told to do the best he could. The attack finally got underway around 5:45 a.m. on October 8, 1918, as the two regiments went "over the top" and attacked German positions to the north and east of Saint-Etienne. Their objective was a road about two kilometers away, certainly not out of reach.

Unfortunately, the advance quickly bogged down; officers were shot, companies became intermingled, and artillery support was poor. Two former Texas National Guard officers managed to rally a group of soldiers, captured several hundred German prisoners, and made it to the road. Once there, however, they realized they were far in advance of any supporting troops. Anticipating a counterattack, the two Texas officers and their men fell back to a slight rise just south of the town. There, the two captains and their men prepared to hunker down for the night and attempted to contact the 141st Infantry on their right and Colonel Bloor's regimental command post. Fortunately, no German counterattack materialized, and the soldiers settled in for the night.

On October 9 and 10, General Whitworth's brigade struggled to advance, but its units were unable to effect any significant change in their positions, mainly because they were still intermingled and knowledge at brigade headquarters as to the troops' frontline positions was inaccurate. The next morning, October 10, General Hulen's Seventy-Second Brigade relieved the Seventy-First Brigade at the same time the Germans began a planned withdrawal to the Aisne River, approximately fifteen miles to the north. The Seventy-Second Brigade led the pursuit of the retreating Germans while Whitworth's Seventy-First Brigade remained at Saint-Etienne to reorganize and resupply.

The attack at Saint-Etienne had not gone well for the Seventy-First Brigade. The 142nd Infantry led the attack, going into the battle with 58 officers and 1,715 men. At its conclusion, 8 officers and 117 men had been killed and 566 had been wounded. The attack certainly suffered from time pressure and lack of preparation, but that was a common experience among AEF units undergoing combat for the first time. The attacking regiment had little time to become acclimated to the front before the attack, and preparations were slow because of the delays getting into the line, numerous meetings between brigade and division headquarters, and the reliance on verbal orders that most certainly changed as they passed from one individual to another. Indeed, the ad hoc way in which the plans for the attack were thrown together would not have boded well for any group of soldiers, no matter how experienced. In sum, the attacking regiment had no clear idea what to do or how to do it. Even so, individuals performed well during the battle, and two of the regiment's soldiers received the Congressional Medal of Honor for their actions that day; nevertheless, the attack was considered a failure. In 1920, the army's Historical Service published a study of the battle of Blanc Mont, which included a chapter on the battle of Saint-Etienne. The study's authors concluded that the Seventy-First Brigade's attack was a failure because of the lack of planning and the lack of written orders. Years later, Colonel George C. Marshall, in scouring World War I battles to illustrate tactical principles in his book on infantry tactics, singled out the attack of the 142nd and their poor timeliness and lack of written orders as examples of what not to do. About the only people who considered the brigade's attack a success were the newspaper reporters back in Texas, one of which, the *Wichita Daily Times*, claimed that the division's contributions to the fighting in the Champagne region was "the most glorious contribution of American military history in this war." Even the *New York Times* seemed impressed, publishing a story titled "Texans Heroic in First Battle."[19]

After Whitworth's brigade was reorganized and resupplied, it advanced north with the rest of the division toward the town of Attigny on the Aisne River. On October 13, the division moved into positions south of the river. Just east of Attigny, the Aisne made a sharp turn to the north before turning back south, creating a horseshoe bend that was occupied by the only German forces on the south bank of the Aisne in a position known as Forest Farm. The German presence was significant because if the Allies captured Attigny, their right flank would be exposed to significant fire from the area of the horseshoe bend. Twice in previous weeks the French had attacked the position and twice been repulsed because of strong defensive fortifications. The German defenses included several belts of barbed wire stretching across the mouth of the bend supported by multiple strong points and dugouts laced with machine guns. General Whitworth's brigade went into positions directly across from Forest Farm, where they remained for nearly two weeks, conducting patrols while enduring rain, artillery fire, and sniper attacks.

In preparation for continuing the advance north of the Aisne River, the French corps commander ordered the Seventy-First Brigade to take the Forest Farm position. Thus, less than three weeks after their first combat at Saint-Etienne, the Seventy-First Brigade received the unenviable task of attacking a fortified position that other forces had twice failed to capture. Planning began on October 24, and the attack took place three days later on October 27. Planners envisioned a twenty-minute rolling artillery barrage followed by a machine gun barrage, while the brigade's two regiments advanced on the German positions. The attack took place as scheduled, beginning at 4:30 p.m. on the afternoon of the twenty-seventh. After the artillery barrage and under cover of the machine gun barrage, the soldiers advanced and within forty-five minutes had completely overrun the enemy's positions. The 142nd Infantry lost eleven men killed and thirty-six wounded, significantly less than their first engagement.[20]

The two battles the Thirty-Sixth Division's Seventy-First Brigade participated in show how the brigade's regiments, much like other combat units in the AEF, learned the difference between warfare that relied on the rifle and maneuver and warfare that employed massive firepower to achieve limited objectives. At Saint-Etienne, the brigade followed the current AEF doctrine, and soldiers who advanced without support were quickly pushed back. At Forest Farm, the soldiers learned from past experiences and adapted their tactics. In fact, both rolling barrages and machine gun barrages were tactics not fully endorsed by AEF headquarters, but they were nevertheless frequently employed by AEF units. In addition, the brigade had more time to prepare, and this allowed the two regiments to use those tactics with a degree of expertise not displayed at Saint-Etienne. For example, proper execution of a rolling barrage allowed soldiers to reach enemy positions before the enemy could get out of their dugouts and into fighting positions after the barrage had passed. The brigade's leaders also had ample time to study the terrain around the position. The assault battalion commander, a captain from Decatur, Texas, named Steve Lillard, had been a company commander at Saint-Etienne and was by all accounts an outstanding combat leader and trusted by his men. As he wrote after the battle, "We had had 24-hours advance notice of this attack, with maps and definite orders. Every man in the organization knew just what he was going to do." Lillard also stressed the cooperation of senior commanders and plentiful artillery support, all of which, he believed, "made it impossible for anything but success."[21]

While the former Texas and Oklahoma National Guardsmen took advantage of the time available to them and adapted their tactics, they also implemented an altogether unique element of warfare that was later successfully employed during World War II. During the fighting at Saint-Etienne, Colonel Bloor and other officers suspected that the Germans were listening in on their communications. To verify this, the division headquarters broadcast coordinates of a false supply dump, and in less than half an hour that area was saturated by a German artillery barrage. The Thirty-Sixth Division then knew it had a problem, but the solution was pure innovation. While many readers will be familiar with the famed Navajo code talkers of World War II, the Texans and Oklahomans of the Thirty-Sixth Division employed the same tactic more than two decades earlier. As regimental commander Colonel Bloor wrote after the armistice, the American Indian soldiers in his regiment spoke twenty-six different languages or dialects, of which only a few had been written down. As Bloor noted, "there was hardly one chance in a million that Fritz [the Germans] would be able to translate these dialects, and the plan to have these Indians transmit telephone messages was adopted."[22]

After deciding to use the Choctaw language, an American Indian soldier was placed in each regiment's command post. The first test occurred the night before the assault on Forest Farm, when the

142nd Infantry used the Choctaw code talkers to withdraw two companies from a frontline position. When that movement was successfully completed, the regiment used the code talkers "repeatedly on the 27th in preparation for the assault on Forest Farm." Colonel Bloor noted that "the enemy's complete surprise" during the attack was "evidence that he could not decipher the messages."[23]

The division's leaders quickly grasped the significance of this innovation. Three days after the battle of Forest Farm, the Thirty-Sixth Division was pulled from the line in preparation for assignment to the American First Army. While waiting to go back to the front, the 142nd held a brief training course to prepare more of their Native American soldiers to transmit messages. To handle the military terminology, they used common Choctaw words such as "big gun" for artillery, "little gun shoot fast," for machine guns, and the battalions were "indicated by one, two, or three grains of corn." Colonel Bloor observed that after the short training, he was confident that if his regiment had gone back into the line, "fine results would have been obtained" by using Choctaw soldiers to transmit messages. Furthermore, he realized that this innovation would allow the use of technology on the battlefield without its limitations: "We were confident the possibilities of the telephone had been obtained without its hazards."[24]

While the two divisions most closely associated with Texas fought bravely on the western front, historian Lonnie J. White made the following comparison between the two Texas–Oklahoma Divisions:

> The 36th made the most of its action-packed stint at the Front from October 7 to 29, 1918, and won high praise for its execution. Comparing its successes in the Champagne region with that of the 90th at St Mihiel the 36th must be given a higher rating, because it succeeded under more adverse circumstances, notably a new commanding general. In addition, it had lost many enlisted men through transfer after reaching France; and it endured a shortage of equipment. The 36th was committed to active combat against dogged resistance immediately upon going into the trenches. In spite of all this, however, the 36th's combat service was too limited for it to be confidently labeled as a crack division, and it never enjoyed more than a short-lived edge over the 90th

as a better fighting machine—if that much, as the 90th was once more in the line, confirming its potential, even before the 36th completed its single tour.[25]

While those are valid points, the two divisions clearly were not in competition with each other. Although the Ninetieth engaged in combat on a much greater scale than the Thirty-Sixth, Texas newspapers continued to focus more of their attention on the Thirty-Sixth Division as opposed to General Allen's division. In fact, the press coverage was so favorable of the Thirty-Sixth Division that some members of the Ninetieth took umbrage at the lack of coverage of their division. One member of the division wrote home, "It sure made me sore to read the papers from home. None of them seems to give the credit to the Ninetieth that it deserves." A Fort Worth soldier wrote, "Nothing against the Thirty-Sixth, but the Ninetieth deserves a little recognition for its work." Finally, Ernest M. Pressley stated it best when he wrote that it seemed "like the people of Texas have forgotten about the fact that the Ninetieth is a Texas Division and it has made a much bigger name and done about ten times as much as the Thirty-Sixth Division."[26]

After weeks of negotiations, the warring parties reached an agreement for an armistice to go into effect on November 11, 1918. On that day, General Allen's Ninetieth Division rested along its frontline positions near the Meuse River, while the Thirty-Sixth Division remained in reserve, training replacements and getting new equipment. Members of both divisions expected the fighting to continue. However, at the appointed time on the now famous "Eleventh hour of the Eleventh day of the Eleventh month," silence descended on the Western Front as the armistice took effect and the fighting ended. Millions of soldiers on both sides of the trenches, including thousands of Texans who were serving on the Western Front, greeted the armistice gratefully. General Smith's Texas Guardsmen realized they would not be going back into the lines, which pleased them as rumors had swirled that the division was going to be used as "shock troops" near Verdun. Fortunately, the armistice laid such rumors to rest. One Thirty-Sixth Division Texan recalled that when his comrades heard the news of the armistice "serious faces that had been drawn for weeks, relaxed and gave vent to smiles and laughter." The villages in which they were housed became places of celebration as buildings and houses were decorated in lights while regimental bands serenaded soldiers and locals alike. On November 12, 1918, members of the Thirty-Sixth Division held a mock funeral for an effigy of the German Kaiser. After the funeral, a regimental band "hit up a lively tune amid cheers." While most soldiers were thankful for the armistice, the *New York Times* quoted a Texas lieutenant as saying, "Well, I don't know but somehow I can't help wondering if we have licked them enough." Seen in the light of later circumstances, such a comment appeared prescient indeed.[27]

The situation was similar in the Ninetieth Division's sector, where men immediately began to ask when they were going home. One Ninetieth Division officer recalled on the night of the armistice that men stood around campfires "talking of home and their part in the World's War." Indeed, after the armistice, many thousands of Texans on the Western Front began to think about those two things. However, bringing home several million men required extensive planning, and General Pershing's AEF staff worked at developing a fair, albeit slow process, and ultimately decided that units would go home in the order in which they arrived overseas. Because it had not arrived in France until August 1918, the Thirty-Sixth would not return home for nearly six months after the armistice in May 1919. That also meant that General Smith's Texans in the Thirty-Sixth Division, and those in many other divisions who were not scheduled to go home soon, would spend Thanksgiving, Christmas, and the New Year in France. To keep their minds off home and holidays, the army provided plenty of things to occupy the AEF, particularly more training.[28]

While the Thirty-Sixth Division moved to a temporary camp near Tonnere to train and await the journey home, General Pershing selected the Ninetieth Division to be part of the U.S. occupation forces in Germany because of its combat record. Under the command of Major General Joseph T. Dickman, the Army of Occupation consisted of ten U.S. Divisions and approximately 470,000 soldiers. Instead of making plans for the trip home, in the last week of November 1918 the Ninetieth Division began its march toward Germany and occupation duty. On December 28, 1918, the Ninetieth Division occupied Daun, Wittlich, and Bernkastel in the *Regierungsbezirk* (administrative region) of Trier, where its troops guarded the railway system within its assigned area of operation. Fortunately, on learning that they were going to Germany instead of going home, many of the men remained in good spirits and one man wrote home that the entire division was eager to see Germany.[29]

In Tonnere, the Thirty-Sixth Division continued a training program to keep the soldiers' minds off the fact that they were not going home anytime soon. As winter moved in, supplies became scarce, and firewood was in short supply. One Texas officer, who had served as a battalion adjutant in the Thirty-Sixth Division, counted his only possessions to be the clothes he wore, his watch and ring, a pen and pocketbook, and a five-dollar bill. More importantly, he also noted the cost of the division's time at the front. In his company only thirty of the 232 men were original members of the organization since Texas. The rest were replacements.[30]

While many Texas soldiers were glad to be finished with the fighting, they soon found the continued training to be an irritant. If the war was over, many asked, why did they continue to train? As one member of the Thirty-Sixth Division observed, while the soldiers were willing to endure any hardship to end the war, once it was over the "work and exercises soon grew uninteresting and tiresome." Another Texan offered a different perspective: "I had rather drill than be on the front for that is a busy place."[31]

As Thanksgiving and Christmas came and went, the soldiers tried to enjoy the holidays, but it was difficult. One Texan wrote home, "You asked me what kind of Christmas I spent. I did not spend any Christmas at all. I did not know when it passed." Another soldier from Abilene remembered it a little more favorably: "It seemed more like Sunday to me than anything else. I sat around the fire almost all day. We sang songs and ran around most all day and had a pretty good time."[32]

As the months wore on, the soldiers of the AEF found other ways to occupy their time. Sports became a favorite outlet for their energy and provided a way to keep them in shape. Football remained particularly popular in the AEF. In fact, when the Texas and Oklahoma regiments were combined back at Camp Bowie in 1917, the regimental commander had used football to strengthen their morale. The AEF followed the same approach, and Texans across the AEF participated, including the Ninetieth Division on occupation duty in Germany. As it turned out, the Thirty-Sixth

Division reached the AEF Championship game, which was held in Paris and attended by General Pershing, many other senior AEF officers, and the king and queen of Belgium. While the Lone Star Division's team played well, the Eighty-Ninth Division secured the victory, 14–6. AEF soldiers also participated in volleyball, basketball, soccer, boxing, and track and field. But athletics was not their only outlet. Texans in the AEF enjoyed theater productions, had access to books and magazines, attended university courses taught by professors at some of the finest universities in Europe, and could visit Paris and the French Riviera while on leave.[33]

In another effort to improve morale, General Pershing ordered each division to design its own insignia to be worn on the shoulder. While this had a practical purpose in making it easier to identify to which unit a soldier belonged, it also strengthened morale. There had been an effort to designate the Ninetieth Division as the "Alamo" Division because it had been organized and trained at San Antonio. And while the nickname generally stuck, General Allen refused to call his organization the Alamo Division because he wanted "the 90th to remain the 90th." Besides, he believed the Alamo nickname would neglect the division's Oklahomans. Instead of an emblem that depicted the Alamo, General Allen approved a "T" and an "O" superimposed over each other, to represent Texas and Oklahoma. As one soldier wrote, "Our division was called the T.O. since it was composed largely of drafted men from Texas and Oklahoma."[34]

Likewise, the Thirty-Sixth Division designed an emblem that included a "T" inside of an arrowhead, the "T" representing the Texans and the arrowhead for the Oklahomans. Later, the Thirty-Sixth was frequently referred to as the Arrowhead Division. During the war, soldiers and civilians also frequently referred to the division as the Panther Division, because of an old nickname of Fort Worth, while the army also nicknamed it the Lone Star Division at one point.[35]

While the army made efforts to keep its soldiers motivated until they could go home, disease, particularly influenza, began to take a toll not only on the AEF but across much of the world as military and civilians alike were swept away by the worldwide epidemic in the fall and winter of 1918–19. In early October 1918, the surgeon general of the army reported more than 13,000 new cases of the flu over a twenty-four-hour period. Although that represented a decrease of 1,000 from the previous day's total, it was still a massive outbreak. Since September 13, 1918, at least 101,733 cases of flu had been reported among soldiers, resulting in more than 2,100 deaths during the same period. By October 10, the *New York Times* reported the number of deaths had reached 6,543 and that the flu raged "unchecked" through most of the army's training camps. Furthermore, the flu had spread to forty-three states and was of epidemic proportions in many of them, including Texas. In the state, three of the four army camps, Bowie, Travis, and Logan, were particularly hard hit, as was the city of San Antonio, which suffered 681 deaths from influenza in 1918–19 and 693 from pneumonia over the same period. Likewise, Houston suffered 542 deaths from flu and 370 from pneumonia, while Dallas suffered 511 influenza deaths and 543 pneumonia deaths over that winter. El Paso suffered 681 flu deaths and 461 pneumonia deaths. Fortunately, with the support of the Red Cross and the YMCA, the scale of the flu epidemic gradually subsided, but not before thousands of soldiers and civilians had perished. The famed Texas writer Katherine Anne Porter's novella *Pale Horse, Pale Rider* is set in Texas during this epidemic.[36]

In the spring of 1919, the Thirty-Sixth Division finally received orders to move to the French port of Brest. On May 31, 1919, the Thirty-Sixth Division arrived in New York, where it remained for one week before beginning their final journey back to Camp Bowie and demobilization. But the trip to Camp Bowie was delayed as the division passed through Oklahoma and paraded in several cities there. As the soldiers traveled across Oklahoma and Texas on their way to Camp Bowie, crowds gathered to watch in every town the trains passed through, and huge crowds awaited their arrival in Fort Worth. By mid- to late June, most of the members of the Thirty-Sixth Division had been demobilized.[37]

Likewise, the last Ninetieth Division units to leave Germany did so on May 22, 1919, and headed for their embarkation ports in France, arriving in Saint-Nazaire just as the Thirty-Sixth Division was departing for the United States. As they departed on various ships for the United States, one member of the Ninetieth wrote that the best way to view France was from the "stern of a ship." Soon, all the division's units were crossing the Atlantic, and two weeks later most had arrived at either Boston, New York, or Newport News, Virginia. The returning division was greeted by crowds numbering in the thousands at the ports, and even the governor of Oklahoma welcomed the Ninetieth Division home in Newport News. Governor Hobby, however, had only sent a representative to welcome home the Texans of the division, and they were far overshadowed by the welcome home given to the Oklahomans. Soon enough, the 357th and 358th Regiments were sent to Camp Pike, Arkansas, for demobilization, while the 359th went to Camp Bowie and the 360th to Camp Travis. While there were welcome home parades in Dallas and other locations for the Ninetieth, the reception for the 360th as it arrived in San Antonio proved to be the largest of them all. After marching from the train station to the Alamo, they stood there in parade formation and listened to the mayor and several others welcome them home and compare them to the men who fought at that famous site.[38]

Upon discharge, every soldier held in his hands a train ticket home, a $60 cash bonus, and discharge papers. Many soldiers visited the sites where they had trained nearly two years early, recalling those early days and what they had experienced over the past two years. What had started back in the summer of 1917 had come to an end as the former soldiers slowly began to make their way home in the summer of 1919, where their communities planned to celebrate their return with homecoming celebrations held in conjunction with Fourth of July parades and picnics. The Texas Doughboys were home at last.[39]

*Chapter 7*

# LEGACIES

As the Texans in the AEF waited to go home, many of them received awards and decorations as a testament of their service. Three Texans received the Medal of Honor in the war, and two more from Oklahoma who had joined the Texas National Guard and served with the Thirty-Sixth Division also received the award. Corporals Samuel Sampler and Harold Turner both received the award for their roles in the fighting around Saint-Etienne in October 1918. Although Sampler joined the Texas National Guard as a resident of Oklahoma, he was an original member of the Texas National Guard's Seventh Texas Infantry. During the advance at Saint-Etienne, Sampler's company received heavy casualties after attempting to advance under machine-gun fire. Sampler managed to locate the German machine guns, and using German grenades, he rushed the position, throwing several of the grenades at the enemy. He killed two German soldiers, silenced the machine gun, and caused twenty-eight enemy soldiers to surrender. His actions allowed his company to continue its advance and led to his nomination for the Medal of Honor.[1]

Harold Turner was also from Oklahoma and an original member of the Seventh Texas. During the fighting around Saint-Etienne on October 8, 1918, Corporal Turner organized a makeshift platoon of scouts, runners, and Signal Corps soldiers. Serving as his platoon's second in command, he led his unit forward under heavy fire. Eventually, casualties reduced the platoon to four men who were pinned down by a machine gun position. When enemy machine-gun fire shifted away from his position, Turner leaped to his feet and rushed the position, which was approximately twenty-five yards away. Using a bayonet, he secured the surrender of fifty German soldiers. As his Medal of Honor citation stated, "his remarkable display of courage and fearlessness was instrumental in destroying the strong point, the fire from which had blocked the advance of his company."[2]

Of the many thousands more Texans who served with the Armed Forces during the war, three others received the Medal of Honor, and hundreds more received decorations for their service. San Antonio native David Bennes Barkley received the Medal of Honor for his actions as a member of the Eighty-Ninth Division. Two days before the November 11th armistice, Barkley volunteered to scout enemy positions near the town of Pouilly, which required his group to swim the Meuse River. Having reached the far bank, the soldiers gathered the information they needed while coming under enemy fire. On their return swim across the river, however, Barkley drowned. The story of David Barkley is of interest because he was a Tejano who was born in Laredo and grew up in San Antonio. Afraid of being put in a segregated unit if he enlisted under his name of Cantú, he enlisted using his father's surname, Barkley. His ethnic background was not publicized until 1989, and he was recognized as the first Hispanic American recipient of the Medal of Honor.[3]

Private Daniel R. Edwards, who joined the army in Bruceville, Texas, was a member of the First Division's Third Machine Gun Battalion. In July 1918, his unit participated in the battle of Soissons. After having spent several weeks in a hospital recovering from previous wounds, Edwards returned to his unit and in the ensuing fighting he crawled into an enemy trench by himself "for the purpose of capturing or killing enemy soldiers known to be concealed therein." Of eight Germans in the trench, he killed four and captured four. While escorting his prisoners to the rear, enemy artillery exploded nearby, killing one of the Germans and shattering one of Edwards's legs, causing him to be evacuated to a hospital once again. According to his Medal of Honor citation, "The bravery of Pfc. Edwards, now a tradition in his battalion because of his previous gallant acts, again caused the morale of his comrades to be raised to high pitch." He received the Medal of Honor in 1923.[4]

Texan David E. Hayden, a U.S. Navy Hospital Apprentice First Class serving with the Second Battalion, Sixth Marine Regiment, received the Medal of Honor for his actions near Thiacourt, France, on September 15, 1918. Cited for "gallantry and intrepidity at the risk of his life above and beyond the call of duty" when a soldier in his unit was mortally wounded by machine-gun fire, Hayden ran without hesitation to the man's assistance. Realizing the man could not be evacuated because of his wounds, Hayden dressed the wounds under intense enemy machine-gun fire before carrying him to a place of safety.[5]

In addition to the Medal of Honor, numerous Texans received the Distinguished Service Cross (DSC) for valor in combat, as well as the French Croix de Guerre, particularly members of the Thirty-Sixth Division, because they served with the French. Approximately eighty-eight members of the Ninetieth Division and at least thirty-nine members of the Thirty-Sixth Division received the Distinguished Service Cross. While it is impossible to describe all the deeds that resulted in the award of the Distinguished Service Cross, several stand out, including Medal of Honor recipient Daniel Edwards, who also received the DSC, as did Private Herbert Dunlavy of the Sixth Marine Regiment, who received the award posthumously for his actions in Belleau Wood in 1918. Laredo resident Captain John L. Taylor and San Antonio native Colonel Hamilton R. Smith, who was killed while commanding the Twenty-Sixth Infantry Regiment, also received the DSC. General Pershing personally presented the DSC to Private Marcelino Serna, a Tejano who was recovering from wounds suffered in combat as a member of the Eighty-Ninth Division.[6]

After the war ended, many physical traces of the war in Texas soon disappeared, primarily because the military build-up happened so quickly and few facilities were built with permanence in mind. In fact, in some cases entire training camps and airfields were gone within a year of the armistice and most had disappeared by the early 1920s. But for those who look, traces of the war can still be seen. In San Antonio, Kelly Field eventually became Kelly Air Force Base, and although it closed in 2001, one can still drive through the area that Captain Benjamin Foulois believed would make a great flying field in 1916. Known today as Port San Antonio, a small set of bungalows that were built in the early 1920s as officer housing are the oldest remaining buildings on the original Kelly Field No. 1, which is still bounded by Leon Creek, the railroad tracks, and the old Frio City road. The airfield is still active and is home to a Texas Air National Guard wing. Likewise, Brooks Field became

Brooks Air Force Base. Although it, too, is now closed, the area is now a public space and contains one of the few remaining World War I–era hangars. And while there are no traces of Camp Travis or the balloon training school at Camp John Wise, Fort Sam Houston remains an active military installation, as do Camps Bullis and Stanley to the northwest of San Antonio.

In Houston, the U.S. Army briefly abandoned Ellington Field after the war, but it was revitalized and is now a Texas Air National Guard base. As for Camp Logan, prominent Texans William C. Hogg and his brother Mike purchased and later turned over more than 1,000 acres of the property to the city of Houston, which established Memorial Park at the location. In Dallas, Love Field is a reminder of the World War I presence in the city and remains a busy hub for air traffic. The state fairgrounds remain, but Camp Dick is only a memory. In nearby Fort Worth, Camp Bowie Boulevard flows through the center of what used to be the base and a small memorial park near the camp headquarters was dedicated in 1950. Little else remains of Camp Bowie, and traces of the city's three airfields are almost non-existent. However, Hulen Street and Hulen Mall are named in honor of General John Hulen, who led the Thirty-Sixth Division's Seventy-Second Brigade during the war. In Waco, the site of Camp MacArthur is noted by a historical marker placed there in 1966. Nothing else remains of that bustling camp or nearby Rich Field. In Wichita Falls, all that remains of Call Field is a road with the same name and a small marker erected by the main gates in 1937 in honor of the men who were killed there in training accidents during the war.[7]

Several other current airfields were named in honor of Texans from the World War I era. For example, the U.S. Air Force named its base in San Angelo in honor of Lieutenant John J. Goodfellow Jr., a native of the city who was killed on the Western Front after dogfighting with German aircraft on September 14, 1918. Likewise, Sheppard Air Force Base in Wichita Falls was named after Senator Morris Sheppard, while Houston's Hobby Airport is named after Texas's wartime governor. In San Antonio, Stinson Field is named for the Stinson family of aviators, one of whom, Eddie Stinson, served as a flight instructor at Kelly Field, while his sister Katherine volunteered to fly for the Air Service but was rejected due to the gender constraints of the day. Instead, she flew from Buffalo, New

York, to Washington, D.C. in support of the Red Cross, among other feats. At the time, her 670-mile flight was described as the "longest aerial flight in a single day that any aviator had made to Washington."[8]

As mentioned throughout this narrative, Texans fought with dozens of AEF units and with the U.S. Navy and Marines Corps. Several served during the war as general officers, and quite a few reached that rank later in their careers. In addition to Texas National Guard general officers such as John Hulen and Henry Hutchings, Texas native Major General William S. Graves, an 1889 West Point graduate, commanded the Eighth Division and led U.S. troops dispatched to Siberia by President Wilson during the war.[9] Brigadier General Andrew Moses was also from Texas, having been born in Burnet in 1874. An 1897 graduate of West Point, he served as Commandant of Cadets at Texas A&M from 1907 to 1911 and during the war commanded the 156th Artillery Brigade of the Eighty-First Division. Before his retirement, he commanded U.S. Army forces in the Pacific from 1937 to 1938. Brigadier General Beaumont Buck was another Texan who served during the war as a general officer, commanding the Twenty-Eighth Infantry Regiment of the First Division. In August 1917, he commanded the division's Second Brigade. Although criticized for his part in the battle of Soissons, Buck was promoted to major general and took command of the Third Division. Other army veterans of World War I from Texas who rose to general officer rank during World War II included George F. Moore, D. B. Netherwood, and John Ashley Warden.[10]

Quite a few army officers from Texas who served in World War I also went on to achieve great success with what would become the U.S. Air Force. That group included such well-known airmen as Claire Lee Chennault, Ira C. Eaker, James E. Fechet, and twins Benjamin and Barney Giles. Chennault, a native of Commerce, later commanded the famous Flying Tigers in the China-Burma-India Theater during World War II. During World War I, he transferred from the infantry to the Air Service and received his wings immediately after the war. Likewise, Ira Eaker, who later commanded the Eighth Air Force and the Mediterranean Allied Air Forces in World War II, was born in Field Creek, Texas, in 1896. He began his career as an infantry officer and learned to fly during the war in Austin and at Kelly Field. The Giles brothers, born in Mineola, both reached general officer rank in World War II, with Barney serving as General Henry H. "Hap" Arnold's deputy commander of the Army Air Forces. His brother Benjamin attended what is now Texas A&M University-Commerce and the University of Texas before training at Ellington Field and then deploying to France in 1918. In the early years of World War II, Benjamin Giles disappeared while on a flight in the Pacific. General James Fechet, who served as chief of the Air Corps from 1927 to 1931, was older than the rest of this group of Texans, having been born at Fort Ringgold in 1877. After serving in the U.S. Cavalry from 1898 to 1918, he commanded San Antonio's Kelly Field in 1918 and finished the war as Air Service Officer of the Southern Department at Fort Sam Houston. Robert Emmet Condon was another example of a Texan who successfully built on his wartime service. Condon, born in Vernon in Wilbarger County in 1896, served in the enlisted ranks until he received his commission in March 1918. During the armistice negotiations, he served as a special advisor to Colonel E. M. House, and in 1920 he became one of the founders of the Junior Chamber of Commerce. He served in the U.S. Air Force until 1954.[11] Other Texans who continued to excel after the war included Major Thomas Barton, who became adjutant general of Texas and unsuccessfully ran for governor; Major Mike Ashburn, who was prominently associated with Texas A&M and the Texas National Guard; Lieutenant Samuel T. Williams, who later commanded the Twenty-Fifth Infantry Division in the Korean War; Ernest O. Thompson, who served on the Texas Railroad Commission; and Corsicana native Beauford H. Jester, who served as governor of Texas from 1947 to 1949.[12]

While the lives of those who participated in the war and who lost their lives on the Western Front or at home because of accidents or sickness may have faded from memory and most of the bases and installations have disappeared, so too did the memories of what the country had been through during the war, particularly in the decades after World War II. In the immediate years after World War I ended, the country celebrated Armistice Day to remember the cataclysmic war that engulfed the world from 1914 to 1918. The nation erected hundreds of memorial parks or statues to honor those who fought in the war, and organizations such as the American Legion were established to commemorate the service of those who fought and to help them with their futures. But over time, the Second World War overshadowed the Great War. In the early 1950s, President Eisenhower changed Armistice Day to Veteran's Day to recognize those who served in all the nation's wars, not just World War I. By the time the 50th anniversary of the war's end came in 1968, many veterans had already passed away and the nation was embroiled in the Vietnam War. Although most of the physical traces of the war in Texas are long gone, the few remaining sites and memorials, no matter how worn, call to mind long ago parades of soldiers marching through the cities and towns of Texas to the cheers of their communities as they headed "over there" to do their part in the "war to end all wars."

World War I was an important and pivotal period in U.S. and Texas history. In his book *Texas and Texans in the Great War*, historian Ralph Wooster points out several ways that the war brought change to the state. First, the implementation of woman's suffrage and Prohibition were crucially important. Although the war was not directly responsible for either of those issues becoming the law of the land, it did play a significant part in generating support for both movements. Wooster also cites the shift from a rural to urban population that began during the war years and the continued rise of industry. Those are certainly valid points, and the evidence clearly supports such assertions of the positive influence of the war on the state in terms of economic impact.[13]

From the political perspective, Wooster also points out that the World War I era witnessed a "changing of the guard" and new political directions in the state as "Old Guard" politicians left public service and younger figures took their places. As he rightly noted, some of those men, such as John Nance Garner, Sam Rayburn, and Morris Sheppard, would play important roles in national politics over the ensuing decades.[14]

In addition to those changes, the war set a precedent in terms of the nation's foreign policy. While the United States had sent troops overseas before, never had the country done so at the scale that it did during World War I. In addition, this was the first time that the National Guard had been mobilized to deploy outside of the United States. Just as importantly, it raised significant questions about the role of the federal government and how much control the government could legitimately exert over its citizens, particularly with the implementation of the first draft since the Civil War and the extent of the federal government's control over moral issues such as Prohibition. It also raised questions of patriotism and loyalty and how foreigners were treated in the United States. The question of border security is another issue that has remained hotly debated into the twenty-first century.

In a different sense, the war served as a transition because the significant military presence in the state that began during the war continued during the twentieth century and into the twenty-first. Although some bases have closed, others have remained major installations for the Department of Defense. This strong military presence within the state through the years has also helped foster the shift from an agricultural state to a more industrialized economy as the number of defense contractors who called Texas home increased.

Thousands of Texas soldiers returned to their lives after they were demobilized in 1919. Many started families and began their professional careers or picked up where they had left off. Of course, as the Great Depression deepened in the 1930s, many veterans faced more difficult times. Some participated in the Bonus March of 1932, and there were those who came back from the war and could not readjust to civilian life. In the early 1920s, the term "shell shock" was used to describe what today is known as post-traumatic stress disorder (PTSD), and there is no doubt that some Texas soldiers suffered significantly after their return from the Western Front. With that being said, the majority of Texas soldiers were able to return home and continue with their lives and achieve some measure of security and well-being for themselves and their families. Nevertheless, the benefits that many white soldiers may have received were not always extended to their fellow comrades in arms who were black or Hispanic.

The fact that the United States claimed to be fighting for democracy around the world led many to question how this would affect the nation's own minorities, particularly blacks and Hispanics. Although many hoped their service would result in respect and equality, it did not bring about significant change in the status of the nation's minorities. As historian Alwyn Barr notes (and using a term often associated with World War II), black Texans hoped for a "Double Victory" in the war, meaning that democracy might be gained in both Europe and the United States. While black Texans participated in parades and rallies and showed their support for the war effort, discrimination in the state remained so prevalent that many migrated north during the war in search of better opportunities. Others, however, stayed in Texas but moved to urban areas in their search for a better life. Out of 31,000 black Texans who were drafted, about 12,000 served in Europe, including some in combat units such as the all-black Ninety-Second and Ninety-Third Divisions. Approximately 240 black Texans lost their lives in combat on the Western Front. Furthermore, African Americans faced significant discriminatory challenges to becoming officers in the U.S. Army at the time, and estimates point to only about seventy black Texans earning commissions during the war. One of those was Carter Wesley, who later achieved prominence as editor of a black newspaper, the *Houston Informer*. And while black Texans could join the U.S. Army, the U.S. Navy only allowed them to enlist as food service workers and the Marines and the new Air Service would not accept black recruits. Barr sums up the war for black Texans in the following way: "For African Americans the war offered mixed results, ranging from frustrations to pride in service and limited gains."[15]

For Hispanic Texans, the war affected them in similar ways. As historian José Ramirez states, Mexican Texans showed both patriotism and disloyalty. Some left the country, not willing to serve, while others served as a way to seek equality and respect. While only about 5,000 of the nearly 200,000 Texans who served in World War I had Spanish surnames, the war nevertheless offered many Hispanics the chance to think of themselves as full Americans rather than as marginal members by society. Indeed, some Hispanic Texans participated in ways that black Texans never could: they served on draft boards, as interpreters, and held patriotic rallies where they had the opportunity to speak out and challenge the very people who had kept them out of full participation in society. But as historian Alexander Mendoza observes, "The end of the Great War did not signify an end to discrimination. . . . The postwar elation and the federal government's awareness of the Mexican American presence in Texas soon gave way to old fashioned stereotypes and prejudices." Nevertheless, although these citizens who fought and died for the United States did not achieve the equality they deserved, the transition had begun.[16]

Many of the political and social questions debated and discussed during the war remain relevant to the United States in the twenty-first century. Although the United States may have expended much more blood and treasure during World War II, Korea, Vietnam, and more recent conflicts, the events that occurred around the world from 1914 to 1918 affected Texans in ways most would never have expected, particularly the more than 5,000 Texans who lost their lives during the most horrific war the world had yet seen.

# Notes

## Chapter 1

*Note*: With the obvious exception of the *New York Times*, the newspapers cited in this book were published in Texas.

[1] Walter L. Buenger *The Path to a Modern South: Northeast Texas between Reconstruction and the Great Depression* (Austin: University of Texas Press, 2001).

[1] Ralph A. Wooster, *Texas and Texans in the Great War* (Buffalo Gap, Tex.: State House Press, 2009), vii.

[3] Richard F. Hamilton and Holger F. Hellwig, *Decisions for War, 1914–1917* (Cambridge, UK: Cambridge University Press, 2004), 225; Wooster, *Texas and Texans in the Great War*, 11.

[4] Jerry M. Cooper, *The Rise of the National Guard: The Evolution of the American Militia, 1863–1920* (Lincoln: University of Nebraska Press, 1997).

[5] Hamilton and Hellwig, *Decisions for War*, 207–208.

[6] Quoted in ibid., 209–211.

[7] Ibid., 209–210; Justus Doenecke, *Nothing Less than War: A New History of America's Entry into World War I* (Lexington: University Press of Kentucky, 2011), 288.

[8] Hamilton and Hellwig, *Decisions for War*, 210–211.

[9] Ibid., 211–212; Doenecke, *Nothing Less than War*, 1.

[10] Hamilton and Hellwig, *Decisions for War*, 212; Doenecke, *Nothing Less than War*, 1.

[11] Hamilton and Hellwig, *Decisions for War*, 216–219.

[12] Historian Justus Doenecke concludes, "Germany forced the administration's hand, doing so at a moment when relations with Berlin were improving and those with London were growing worse. When U-boats began sinking American vessels without rescuing their crews, Wilson had run out of options." See Doenecke, *Nothing Less Than War*, 307.

[13] Hamilton and Hellwig, *Decisions for War*, 213, 220–223.

[14] Ibid., 222; Tom Connally, *My Name is Tom Connally* (New York: Thomas Y. Crowell, 1954), 78–81; Wooster, *Texas and Texans in the Great War*, 31–32.

[15] Woodrow Wilson, "Address to a Joint Session of Congress Requesting a Declaration of War Against Germany," <http://www.presidency.ucsb.edu/ws/index.php?pid=65366&st=&st1> [Accessed Mar. 20, 2017].

[16] Hamilton and Hellwig, *Decisions for War*, 222; Connally, *My Name is Tom Connally*, 78–81.

[17] Wooster, *Texas and Texans in the Great War*, 20–21.

[18] David Montejano, *Anglos and Mexicans in the Making of Texas, 1836–1986* (Austin: University of Texas Press, 1987), 117–122; Charles H. Harris III and Louis R. Sadler, *The Texas Rangers and the Mexican Revolution: The Bloodiest Decade, 1910–1920* (Albuquerque: University of New Mexico Press, 2004), 210–213, 263; *Abilene Reporter*, Apr. 10–11, 1917; Wooster, *Texas and Texans in the Great War*, 20–21. A recent account of the WWI-era military build-up in Texas can be found in Thomas T. Smith, *The Old Army in the Big Bend of Texas: The Last Cavalry Frontier, 1911–1921* (Austin: Texas State Historical Association, 2018).

[19] Wooster, *Texas and Texans in the Great War*, 25–26. The National Defense Act of 1916 reorganized the militia and helped professionalize it during this period. Another significant aspect of the Punitive Expedition was the nation's first use of military aviation in a campaign. The army had formed the First Aero Squadron at Texas City, Texas, in 1913, and while stationed at Fort Sam Houston in 1916 the squadron deployed to support General Pershing's expedition. Under the command of Captain Benjamin D. Foulois, First Aero Squadron airmen experimented with this new capability on the battlefield for the first time. Although the aircraft were not suitable for the rough conditions they encountered, the airmen did what they could to keep them flying and provide useful reconnaissance and courier services for General Pershing's forces. While technological limitations kept the squadron from performing as they had hoped, Foulois would return to Texas late in 1916 and play an important part in bringing military aviation to the state. The most recent and best work on the National Guard's mobilization on the border is Charles H. Harris III and Louis R. Sadler, *The Great Call-Up: The Guard, the Border, and the Mexican Revolution* (Norman: University of Oklahoma Press, 2015).

[20] *Dallas Morning News*, Mar. 2, 1917; *Denton Record-Chronicle*, Mar. 3, 1917; *The Abilene Reporter*, Apr. 6, 1917; *Wichita Daily Times*, Mar. 1, 1917; Doenecke, *Nothing Less than War*, 268.

[21] Thomas Boghardt, *The Zimmermann Telegram: Intelligence, Diplomacy, and America's Entry into World War I* (Annapolis, Md.: Naval Institute Press, 2012); Wooster, *Texas and Texans in the Great War*, 30–31.

[22] *New York Times*, July 17, Nov. 15, Dec. 3, 4, 26, 27, 28, 1917, and Jan. 4, 26, Mar. 2, Apr. 11, 16, 1918; *Dallas Morning News*, Mar. 2, 1917; *Austin American Statesman*, Mar. 1, 1917. See also *Houston Post*, Apr. 7, 1917. The March 1, 1917, edition of the *Austin American Statesman* described alleged German submarine bases along the Gulf Coast. Whether true or not, these reports helped stoke plenty of anti-German sentiment. In fact, the tension along the border was strong enough that Governor James Ferguson feared that Texas would be the first to suffer if Mexico allied itself with Germany and the Triple Alliance. He compared the possible fate of Texas to that of Belgium, which had suffered heavily from German reprisals in 1914.

[23] *New York Times*, Jan. 26, 1918. The division consisted of nine regiments of cavalry, including the Fifth, Seventh, and Eighth in El Paso, the First, Fifteenth, and Seventeenth in Douglas, Arizona, and the Sixth, Thirteenth, and Sixteenth in San Antonio.

[24] Hamilton and Hellwig, *Decisions for War*, 207, 211–212. See also John Milton Cooper, *Pivotal Decades: The United States, 1900–1920* (New York: W.W. Norton, 1990) and Arthur S. Link, *Woodrow Wilson and the Progressive Era, 1910–1917* (New York: Harper and Row, 1954).

## Chapter 2

[1] For excellent overviews of the military history of the state, see Alexander Mendoza and Charles David Grear (eds.), *Texans and War: New Interpretations of the State's Military History* (College Station: Texas A&M University Press, 2012), 1–13, and Joseph G. Dawson III (ed.), *The Texas Military Experience: From the Texas Revolution through World War II* (College Station: Texas A&M University Press, 1995).

[2] Wooster, *Texas and Texans in the Great War*, 12–13.

[3] Ibid., 12–13, 16.

[4] Ibid., 16–17, 39.

[5] Ibid., 12.

[6] Ibid., 13, 54.

[7] *New York Times*, Dec. 12, 1917; Kenneth E. Hendrickson Jr., *The Chief Executives of Texas* (College Station: Texas A&M University Press, 1995), 119–167; Wooster, *Texas and Texans in the Great War*, 10.

[8] *New York Times*, Aug. 8, 1918.

[9] *New York Times*, July 28, 1918, and May 17, 1919. The members of the delegation who were defeated in the primary included Atkins "Jeff" McLemore, Joe Eagle, Alexander W. Gregg, Rufus Hardy, and Sam Rayburn. James L. Slayden pulled out of the race before the primary because President Wilson had sent a telegram to people in the state that accused Slayden of not supporting his administration. See *New York Times*, July 28, 1918.

[10] *Congressional Record, Containing the Proceedings and Debates of the First Session of the Sixty-Fifth Congress of the United States of America* (hereafter cited as *Congressional Record, Sixty-Fifth Congress*), Vol. 55 (Washington, D.C.: Government Printing Office, 1917), part 1, 155, 193, 930; part 2, 55, 1451; part 3, 2428; 2270; part 4, 3994; part 5, 4396; part 6, 5572, 5785; part 7, 7323; *New York Times*, June 21, Aug. 2, 1917; *Abilene Reporter*, Apr. 6, 9, 11, 1917; Robert L. Wagner, "Culberson, Charles Allen," *The Handbook of Texas Online*, <http://www.tshaonline.org/handbook/online/articles/fcu02> [Accessed Mar. 5, 2016]; Richard Bailey, "Sheppard, John Morris," *The Handbook of Texas Online*, <http://www.tshaonline.org/handbook/online/articles/fsh24> [Accessed Mar. 5, 2016]; *New York Times*, June 21, 1917; Wooster, *Texas and Texans in the Great War*, 72–73.

[11] *Congressional Record, Sixty-Fifth Congress*, part 1, 663; part 4, 3903; part 8, appendix, 348. The Texas Delegation to the House of Representatives included Eugene Black, James Young, Sam Rayburn, Hatton Sumner, Rufus Hardy, Tom Connally, Marvin Jones, John Nance Garner, Atkins "Jeff" McLemore, Martin Dies, Alexander W. Gregg, Joe Eagle, Joseph Mansfield, James P. Buchanan, James C. Wilson, James L. Slayden, Thomas L. Blanton, and Daniel E. Garrett. Of course, Sam Rayburn would go on to have a significant influence on Lyndon B. Johnson, and John Nance Garner later served as vice president under Franklin D. Roosevelt. Thomas L. Blanton was the brother of Annie Webb Blanton, the first woman to hold elected office in Texas. In 1918, Blanton got into a brief fistfight with fellow congressman J. C. Wilson because of a voting agreement over a prohibition measure that each man claimed the other had violated. See *New York Times*, June 28, Aug. 24, 1918; Wooster, *Texas and Texans in the Great War*, 71–76.

[12] *Congressional Record, Sixty-Fifth Congress*, part 1, 150, 261, 385; *San Antonio Express*, Apr. 6, 1917.

[13] *Congressional Record, Sixty-Fifth Congress*, part 1, 261, 385–386, 413; *San Antonio Express*, Apr. 6, 1917.

[14] *Congressional Record, Sixty-Fifth Congress*, part 1, 357–358.

[15] Historian Justus Doenecke described McLemore as a "former cowboy, gold prospector, and newspaperman who for some curious reason placed a colon between his first and last names (i.e. Jeff:McLemore)." See Doenecke, *Nothing Less than War*, 159.

[16] *Congressional Record, Sixty-Fifth Congress*, part 8, appendix, 29; *Houston Post*, Apr. 7, 1917; Wooster, *Texas and Texans in the Great War*, 71.

[17] *Houston Post*, Apr. 7, 1917.

[18] *Congressional Record, Sixty-Fifth Congress*, part 8, Appendix, 29; Lewis L. Gould, *Progressives and Prohibitionists: Texas Democrats in the Wilson Era* (reprint; Austin: Texas State Historical Association, 1992), 163–165, 243–244; *New York Times*, Nov. 5, 1917, and July 31, 1918; Doenecke, *Nothing Less than War*, 159–165; Wooster, *Texas and Texans in the Great War*, 24–25.

[19] Doenecke, *Nothing Less than War*, 5–6; Wooster, *Texas and Texans in the Great War*, 61–65. See also Charles Neu, *Colonel House: A Biography of Woodrow Wilson's Silent Partner* (New York: Oxford University Press, 2015).

[20] *New York Times*, July 29, 1917; Wooster, *Texas and Texans in the Great War*, 32, 51–52, 65–71. On Burleson, see Adrian Anderson, "President Wilson's Politician: Albert Sidney Burleson," in *Texas Vistas: Selections from the Southwestern Historical Quarterly*, ed. Ralph A. Wooster and Robert A. Calvert (rev. ed.; Austin: Texas State Historical Association Press, 1987), 271–286. Lovett's son, Robert A. Lovett, born in Huntsville in 1895, gained flying experience as a naval ensign during World War I, and later served with great distinction as the assistant secretary of air in the administration of Franklin D. Roosevelt, where he oversaw the massive expansion of the U.S. Army Air Forces. He culminated his career as the fourth secretary of defense, serving from 1951–1953.

[21] Hamilton and Hellwig, *Decisions for War*, 222; *Houston Post*, Apr. 7, 1917; *Journal of the House of Representatives of the Second Called Session of the Thirty-Fifth Legislature* (Austin: Von Boeckmann-Jones Co., 1917), 36–37; *Journal of the House of Representative of the Regular Session of the Thirty-Sixth Legislature, convened January 14, 1919, and adjourned March 19, 1919* (Austin: Von Boeckman-Jones, 1919), 76–77.

## Chapter 3

[1] See John Garry Clifford, *The Citizen Soldiers: The Plattsburg Training Camp Movement, 1913–1920* (new ed.; Lexington: University Press of Kentucky, 2014).

[2] *San Antonio Express*, Apr. 6, 1917. The citizens of San Antonio had presented Pershing a "pet golden eagle" as a mascot for his expedition into Mexico in search of Pancho Villa back in 1916. See *New York Times*, Feb. 18, 1918.

[3] *Denton Record-Chronicle*, Mar. 29, Apr. 6, 1917; *Houston Post*, Apr. 7, 1917; *Amarillo Daily News*, Apr. 7, 1917; *Journal of the House of Representatives of the Second Called Session of the Thirty-Fifth Legislature*, 36–37; *Wise County Messenger*, Apr. 6, 20, 1917; *San Antonio Express*, Apr. 7, 1917; *Houston Post*, Apr. 7, 1917; *Fort Worth Record*, Apr. 5, 1917.

[4] *Wise County Messenger*, Apr. 6, 20, 1917; *San Antonio Express*, Apr. 7, 1917; *Houston Post*, Apr. 7, 1917.

[5] *Wise County Messenger*, Apr. 18, 1917, *Dallas Morning News*, Apr. 19, 1917;

*Abilene Reporter,* Apr. 8, 24, 1917; *Houston Post,* Apr. 7, 1917; *San Antonio Express,* Apr. 6, 1917.

⁶ *Wise County Messenger,* Apr. 18, 1917, *Dallas Morning News,* Apr. 19, 1917; *Abilene Reporter,* Apr. 8, 24, 1917; *Houston Post,* Apr. 7, 1917.

⁷ *Fort Worth Record,* Apr. 5, 1917; *Abilene Reporter* Apr. 9, 11, 1917; Lonnie J. White, *The 90th Division in World War I: The Texas-Oklahoma Draft Division in the Great War* (Manhattan, Kans.: Sunflower University Press, 1996), 45.

⁸ *San Antonio Express,* Apr. 6, 1917; *New York Times,* May 1, 1917.

⁹ *Dallas Morning News,* June 8, 1917; *Wichita Daily Times,* May 13, 16, and June 6, 1917; *Gainesville Daily Register,* June 21, 1917; *Cleburne Daily Enterprise,* May 3, 16, 1917; *Amarillo Daily News,* June 12, 1917; *San Antonio Express,* Apr. 6, 1917; *Houston Post,* Apr. 7, 1917; *New York Times,* Oct. 20, 1917, and May 3, 1918; Wooster, *Texas and Texans in the Great War,* 103.

¹⁰ *Dallas Morning News,* May 11, 15, 1917; *Wise County Messenger,* July 20, 1917; Ronald Schaffer, *America in the Great War: The Rise of the Welfare State* (New York: Oxford University Press, 1991), 18; Wooster, *Texas and Texans in the Great War,* 98.

¹¹ *Dallas Morning News,* May 11, June 8, Sep. 12, 1917; *Wichita Daily Times,* July 26, 1917; *Gainesville Daily Register,* June 25, 1917; *Cleburne Daily Enterprise,* July 17, 1917; *New York Times,* Oct. 9, 1917, and May 5, 1918.

¹² *New York Times,* May 25, 1917, Mar. 31, May 26, June 26, 1918; *Houston Post,* Apr. 7, 1917; *Fort Worth Record,* Apr. 25, 1917; *Dallas Morning News,* Apr. 22, June 8, 1917; *Amarillo Daily News,* Apr. 15, 1917; *Cleburne Enterprise,* May 20, 1917; Wooster, *Texas and Texans in the Great War,* 56–59.

¹³ *New York Times,* June 26, 1917, and May 12, July 4, 1918; Wooster, *Texas and Texans in the Great War,* 52–53.

¹⁴ *New York Times,* May 19, 1917.

¹⁵ Ibid., June 15, 1917.

¹⁶ Ibid., Oct. 9, 18, 1917, and May 9, 1918; Wooster, *Texas and Texans in the Great War,* 92. In a rather unique effort to support the war, the residents of Poolville, west of Fort Worth, raised $1,246 as a reward in a bid to capture Kaiser Wilhelm and deliver him "into the hands of the American authorities." As the *New York Times* noted, "Practically every male resident of the town contributed to the fund." The reward, obviously, was never claimed. *New York Times,* May 5, 1918.

¹⁷ Ralph W. Steen, "World War I," *The Handbook of Texas Online,* <https://tshaonline.org/handbook/online/articles/qdw01> [Accessed Apr. 23, 2016]; *Order of Battle of the United States Land Forces in the World War: American Expeditionary Forces: Divisions* (3 vols., 1931; reprint, Washington, D.C.: Government Printing Office, 1988), II, 933; *New York Times,* May 21 and June 26, 1917.

¹⁸ *Houston Post,* Apr. 7, 1917; *New York Times,* July 14, 1918.

¹⁹ *Houston Post,* Apr. 7, 1917; Wooster, *Texas and Texans in the Great War,* 101–104; Melanie A. Kirkland, "Texas Women at War," in Mendoza and Grear, *Texans and War,* 72–75. Because of the presence of so many thousands of men in cities with training camps, the Young Women's Christian Association (YWCA) developed "active plans for the protection, comfort and happiness of girls in the city." According to a San Antonio newspaper, local YWCA committees planned for the "recreation and care of the girls," and developed locations where mothers and sisters of soldiers could come and stay while visiting their sons, brothers or husbands in training camps. *San Antonio Express,* Aug. 17, 1917.

[20] An outstanding work is the publication of the World War I diary of José de la Luz Saenz in English. This work highlights the experiences of an insightful individual who believed that the war could be used by Hispanics to bolster their position in society. See Emilio Zamora (ed.), *The World War I Diary of José de la Luz Saenz* (College Station: Texas A&M University Press, 2014).

[21] *Gainesville Daily Register*, Apr. 18, 1917.

[22] *Cleburne Daily Enterprise*, May 4, 1917, and June 1, 1917; *Wichita Daily Times*, Apr. 13, 20, 1917.

[23] *New York Times*, July 31, 1917; Garna L. Christian, *Black Soldiers in Jim Crow Texas, 1899–1917* (College Station: Texas A&M University Press, 1995), 128–145.

[24] Christian, *Black Soldiers in Jim Crow Texas*, 145–172.

[25] Ibid., 145–172; Robert V. Haynes, "Houston Riot of 1917," *The Handbook of Texas Online*, <http://www.tshaonline.org/handbook/online/articles/jcho4> [Accessed April 30, 2016].

[26] Christian, *Black Soldiers in Jim Crow Texas*, 145–172; Haynes, "Houston Riot of 1917."

[27] *Wichita Daily Times*, Aug. 26, 1917; Christian, *Black Soldiers in Jim Crow Texas*, 177; Robert V. Haynes, "The Houston Mutiny and Riot of 1917," in Wooster and Calvert, *Texas Vistas*, 287–302.

[28] *Wichita Daily Times*, Apr. 8, 1917.

[29] *Dallas Morning News*, Apr. 4, 7, 1917; *Abilene Reporter*, Apr. 8, 10, 1917; *Cleburne Daily Enterprise*, July 27, and Sep. 6, 1917; *Quanah Tribune Chief*, July 5, 1917; *New York Times*, Nov. 27, 1917.

[30] *New York Times*, Nov. 11, 1917, Jan. 20, 1918; *Wichita Daily Times*, Apr. 8, 1917.

[31] *Houston Post*, Apr. 7, 1917; Wooster, *Texas and Texans in the Great War*, 66–68.

[32] *Amarillo Daily News*, Apr. 7, 15, 24, 1917; *Wichita Daily Times*, Apr. 6, 1917.

[33] *Amarillo Daily News*, Apr. 17, 1917; *Wichita Daily Times*, Apr. 8, 15, 19, and June 3, 1917.

[34] *Amarillo Daily News*, Apr. 8, 1917; *Houston Post*, Apr. 7, 1917; *New York Times*, June 25, 1917, Feb. 14, and Mar. 15, 1918.

[35] *Dallas Morning News*, Apr. 4, 7, 1917; *Abilene Reporter*, Apr. 8, 10, 1917; *Cleburne Daily Enterprise*, July 27, and Sep. 6, 1917; *Quanah Tribune Chief*, July 5, 1917; *New York Times*, Nov. 27, 1917. There was even a fear that German chemists were manufacturing a poison made from a plant that grew in Texas and Mexico and then shipping the poison back to Germany. When three "chemists" were arrested while trying to cross the border into the United States at Laredo, the "plot" was exposed. See *New York Times*, July 19, 1917; *New York Times*, June 25, 1917, Feb. 14, and Mar. 15, 1918.

[36] *New York Times*, July 6, 1917.

[37] *Report of the Proceedings of the Second Congress of the Pan-American Federation of Labor* (n.p., 1919), 3–10.

[38] *New York Times*, July 6, 1917, June 17, 1918, and Nov. 14, 1918.

[39] James O. Kievit and Brent C. Bankus, "Defending the Homeland during World War I: The U.S. Guards, 1917–1919," *On Point: The Journal of Army History* 21 (Spring 2016): 36–43.

[40] Ibid., 36–43.

## Chapter 4

[1] White, *90th Division in World War I*, 2.

[2] John Whiteclay Chambers, *To Raise an Army: The Draft Comes to Modern America* (New York: The Free Press, 1987), 79, 103, 105, 128.

[3] Ibid., 130, 133.

[4] *Congressional Record, Sixty-Fifth Congress*, part 2, 1283–1284, 1484–1485; Connally, *My Name is Tom Connally*, 91.

[5] *Houston Post*, Apr. 7, 1917.

[6] *Congressional Record, Sixty-Fifth Congress*, part 8, appendix, 120–122, 125; part 1, 256, 450, 562; *Cleburne Daily Enterprise*, May 8, 1917; *San Antonio Express*, Apr. 6, 1917.

[7] *Congressional Record, Sixty-Fifth Congress*, part 2, 1233–1235; *Wichita Daily Times*, Apr. 23, 25, 1917; Wooster, *Texas and Texans in the Great War*, 36.

[8] *Wichita Daily Times*, Apr. 11, July 16, 1917; *Gainesville Daily Register*, Apr. 10, 1917; Wooster, *Texas and Texans in the Great War*, 36.

[9] *New York Times*, June 6, 1917, and Jan. 20, 1918; Enoch H. Crowder, *Second Report of the Provost Marshall General to the Secretary of War on the Operations of the Selective Service System to December 20, 1918* (Washington, D.C.: Government Printing Office, 1919), 268, 364–365, 479; Wooster, *Texas and Texans in the Great War*, 39. For a local study of how the draft operated in one Texas county, see Gregory W. Ball, "Denton County, Texas, and the Draft During the First World War," in Richard B. McCaslin, Donald E. Chipman, and Andrew J. Torget (eds.), *This Corner of Canaan: Essays in Honor of Randolph B. Campbell* (Denton: University of North Texas Press, 2013), 335–359.

[10] *San Antonio Express*, Aug. 17, 1917; *New York Times*, Sep. 14, 1917.

[11] Crowder, *Second Report*, 277; *Gainesville Daily Register*, June 29, 1917.

[12] *Abilene Reporter*, June 5, 1917; *Cleburne Daily Enterprise*, June 6, 1917.

[13] *New York Times*, June 6, 1917, and Jan. 20, 1918; White, *90th Division in World War I*, 19.

[14] *Wichita Daily Times*, May 31, 1917; *Denton Record-Chronicle*, June 1, 2, 4, 1917; *New York Times*, Aug. 10, 1917.

[15] *Dallas Morning News*, May 20, 1917; *New York Times*, June 3, Sep. 25, 1917.

[16] *Dallas Morning News*, Sep. 10, 1917, and Oct. 19, 1917, *New York Times*, May 29, 1917. Bryant, Risley, and Powell were granted bond for $10,000 each in March 1918, although none could pay it. See *Dallas Morning News*, Mar. 10, 1918. For more on the FLPA, see Jeanette Keith, *Rich Man's War, Poor Man's Fight* (Chapel Hill: University of North Carolina Press, 2004), 87–101.

[17] *San Antonio Express*, Aug. 17, 1917; *New York Times*, Sep. 16, 1917, and July 14, 1918. In addition to the band leader, military authorities at Camp Travis convicted forty-five members of the Mennonite religion of disloyalty and sentenced them to life imprisonment commuted to twenty-five-years each to be served at Fort Leavenworth, Kansas. See *New York Times*, June 11, 1918.

[18] *Denton Record-Chronicle*, Aug. 16, 1918; *Cleburne Daily Enterprise*, July 23, 1917; *Amarillo Daily News*, June 16, 1917; *Fort Worth Record*, June 13, 17, 1917; *New York Times*, Jan. 20, 1918.

[19] Crowder, *Second Report*, 479.

[20] Ibid., 279–280, ix–x; *New York Times*, Jan. 20, 1918.

[21] Crowder, *Second Report*, 586–588.

[22] *Amarillo Daily News*, June 16, 1917, and May 25, 31, 1917.

[23] Wooster, *Texas and Texans in the Great War*, 122–123.

[24] *Amarillo Daily News*, Apr. 12, 19, and May 2, 1917; *Wichita Daily Times*, June 21, 1917, and Aug. 20, 1917; *Fort Worth Record*, May 30, 1917; *Dallas Morning News*, Aug. 6, 1917, *Houston Post*, Apr. 7, 1917; *New York Times*, July 7, Aug. 28, 1917.

[25] *Wichita Daily Times*, June 28, 1917.

[26] Lonnie J. White, *Panthers to Arrowheads: The 36th (Texas-Oklahoma) Division in World War I* (Austin: Presidial Press, 1984), 1–2, 5. For an overview of National Guard reform see Cooper, *Rise of the National Guard*, 108–127.

[27] White, *Panthers to Arrowheads*, 1–2, 5; *San Antonio Express*, Apr. 6, 1917; *Houston Post*, Apr. 7, 1917.

[28] White, *Panthers to Arrowheads*, 6–8; *Wichita Daily Times*, June 4, 1917; *Dallas Morning News*, June 26, 1917.

[29] "Instructions for the use of those designated as officers of proposed organizations of the National Guard of Texas," undated, 36th Division Association Papers, Hulen Correspondence, 1916–1917 (Archives Division, Texas State Library, Austin); *Cleburne Daily Enterprise*, July 11–12, 1917; *Abilene Reporter*, June 18, 1917, and July 20, 1917; *Amarillo Daily News*, July 25, 1923; *Wichita Daily Times*, Apr. 15, and June 13, 15, 17, 21, 29, 1917.

[30] General Orders No. 2, June 15, 1917, 36th Division Association Papers, Hulen Correspondence; *Dallas Morning News*, July 7, 9, 1917; *New York Times*, Jan. 20, 1918; White, *90th Division in World War I*, 19. Oklahoma's adjusted draft quota was 15,564. See White, *90th Division in World War I*, 25.

[31] *Wichita Daily Times*, June 21, 1917.

[32] *Gainesville Daily Register*, June 19, 22, and July 2, 1917; *Wichita Daily Times*, July 1, 5, 8, 16, 1917; Charles H. Barnes, *History of the 142nd Infantry of the Thirty-Sixth Division: October 15, 1917, to June 17, 1919* (Blackwell, Okla.: Blackwell Job Printing Company, 1922), 18; *New York Times*, June 15, July 1, 1917.

[33] *New York Times*, Sept. 19, 1918; Wooster, *Texas and Texans in the Great War*, 39.

## Chapter 5

[1] *Order of Battle of the United States Land Forces in the World War: Zone of the Interior: Territorial Department, Tactical Divisions Organized in 1918, Posts, Camps, and Stations* (3 vols., 1949; reprint, Washington, D.C.: Government Printing Office, 1988), III, part 2, 602.

[2] Ibid., 602–603, 606–608, 614; Julia Cauble Smith, "Camp Holland," *The Handbook of Texas Online*, <http://www.tshaonline.org/handbook/online/articles/qbc13> [Accessed Mar. 7, 2016].

[3] *Order of Battle of the United States Land Forces in the World War*, III, pt. 2, 602–603, 614.

[4] Ibid., 606–608.

[5] *Order of Battle of the United States Land Forces in the World War*, III, pt. 2, 903, 904, 907, 910–911, 927, 933; *New York Times*, Nov. 17, 1917; Wooster, *Texas and Texans in the Great War*, 46.

[6] *Order of Battle of the United States Land Forces in the World War*, III, pt. 2, 903, 904, 907, 910–911, 923, 925; Leon C. Metz, *Desert Army: Fort Bliss on the Texas Border* (El Paso: Mangan Books, 1988).

[7] *Order of Battle of the United States Land Forces in the World War*, II, 5.

[8] *Gainesville Daily Register*, June 19, 22, and July 2, 1917; *Wichita Daily Times*, July 1, 5, 8, 16, 1917; Barnes, *History of the 142nd Infantry of the Thirty-Sixth Division*, 18; *New York Times*, June 15, July 1, 1917.

[9] *Report of the Acting Chief of the Militia Bureau, 1918* (Washington, D.C.: Government Printing Office, 1919), 120, 122–123, 152; White, *90th Division in World War I*, 3; *Albany News*, Sep. 28, 1917.

[10] White, *90th Division in World War I*, 3; *Order of Battle of the United States Land Forces in the World War*, III, pt. 2, 913–914, 926.

[11] *Order of Battle of the United States Land Forces in the World War*, III, pt. 2, 931–933. For reviews of the construction at Camp Travis, see White, *90th Division in World War I*, 6–13; and John M. Manguso, *San Antonio in the Great War* (Charleston, S.C.: Arcadia, 2014), 7–10.

[12] *Order of Battle of the United States Land Forces in the World War*, III, pt. 2, 917; *New York Times*, June 3, 1917.

[13] White, *Panthers to Arrowhead*, 15–16; *San Antonio Express*, Apr. 6, 1917; Claudia Hazlewood, "Camp Logan," *The Handbook of Texas Online*, <http://www.tshaonline.org/handbook/online/articles/qcc26> [Accessed May 2, 2016]; Vivian Elizabeth Smyrl, "Camp MacArthur," *The Handbook of Texas Online*, <http://www.tshaonline.org/handbook/online/articles/qcc27> [Accessed May 2, 2016]; *Order of Battle of the United States Land Forces in the World War*, II, 179; Steen, "World War I"; Mel Brown, *Wings Over San Antonio* (Charleston, S.C.: Arcadia, 2001), 1–102.

[14] *Order of Battle of the United States Land Forces in the World War*, III, pt. 2, 903, 916, 926.

[15] Ibid., 934–935.

[16] Ibid., 923.

[17] White, *Panthers to Arrowheads*, 16–19; White, *90th Division in World War I*, 3; Steen, "World War I"; J'Nell Pate, *Arsenal of Defense: Fort Worth's Military Legacy* (Denton: Texas State Historical Association, 2011).

[18] White, *Panthers to Arrowheads*, 16–19; White, *90th Division in World War I*, 3.

[19] *Order of Battle of the United States Land Forces in the World War*, III, pt. 2, 900–902; *New York Times*, Oct. 14, 1917; White, *Panthers to Arrowheads*, 40, 42–43.

[20] *Order of Battle of the United States Land Forces in the World War*, III, pt. 2, 898, 904, 930. See also Bill Leary, *Flyers of Barron Field: A Chronicle of the Wild Antics of Flyers Stationed around Fort Worth in World War I* (Fort Worth: Yrael Publishing, 2003).

[21] Steen, "World War I"; *New York Times*, Aug. 7, 30, Nov. 18, 1917.

[22] *Order of Battle of the United States Land Forces in the World War*, III, pt. 2, 907–908, 920; Steen, "World War I"; *New York Times*, Dec. 9, 1918.

[23] *Albany News*, Sep. 28, 1917.

[24] *Order of Battle of the United States Land Forces in the World War*, III, pt. 2, 919–920; *Order of Battle of the United States Land Forces in the World War*, II, 195.

[25] *Order of Battle of the United States Land Forces in the World War*, III, pt. 2, 909–910, 913; Hazlewood, "Camp Logan"; Steen, "World War I."

[26] *Order of Battle of the United States Land Forces in the World War*, III, pt. 2, 924.

[27] Smyrl, "Camp MacArthur"; *Order of Battle of the United States Land Forces in the World War*, II, 179; *Order of Battle of the United States Land Forces in the World War*, III, pt. 2, 920–921; *Albany News*, Sep. 28, 1917.

[28] *Albany News*, Sep. 28, 1917; Steen, "World War I"; *Order of Battle of the United States Land Forces in the World War*, III, pt. 2, 921–922, 925, 933.

[29] *Order of Battle of the United States Land Forces in the World War*, III, pt. 2, 903–904; Wooster, *Texas and Texans in the Great War*, 46.

[30] Kenneth Baxter Ragsdale, *Wings Over the Mexican Border: Pioneer Military Aviation in the Big Bend* (Austin: University of Texas Press, 1984).

[31] *Order of Battle of the United States Land Forces in the World War*, III, pt. 2, 906–907, 927.

[32] *New York Times*, Sep. 4, 1917.

[33] White, *90th Division in World War I*, 15.

[34] Timothy K. Nenninger, "Unsystematic as a Mode of Command: Commanders and the Process of Command in the American Expeditionary Forces, 1917–1918," *Journal of Military History* 64 (July 2000): 739–768.

[35] Lonnie White, "Chief of the Arrowheads: Major General William R. Smith and the 36th Division in France, 1918–1919," *Military History of Texas and the Southwest* 16, No. 3 (1982): 149–176. In addition to the removal of Greble, Texas National Guard Colonel Jules Muchert of Sherman lost his command of the 144th Infantry presumably because of his German background; Wooster, *Texas and Texans in the Great War*, 126.

[36] Allen was late getting to New York to catch the liner taking the group of generals to France and he had to charter a yacht to catch up to the ocean liner. On the rest of the trip, he endured the good-natured kidding of his fellow general officers. See White, *90th Division in World War I*, 40.

[37] Lonnie J. White, "Allen, Henry Tureman," *The Handbook of Texas Online*, <http://www.tshaonline.org/handbook/online/articles/fal76> [Accessed May 11, 2016]; *Order of Battle of the United States Land Forces in the World War*, II, 408; *San Antonio Express*, Aug. 17, 1917; White, *90th Division in World War I*, 13–14, 29, 40–41; Lonnie J. White, "Camp Travis," *The Handbook of Texas Online*, <http://www.tshaonline.org/handbook/online/articles/qbc28> [Accessed Apr. 26, 2016].

[38] Gregory W. Ball, *They Called Them Soldier Boys: A Texas Infantry Regiment in World War I*. (Denton: University of North Texas Press, 2013). For an excellent overview of the training that World War I soldiers conducted, see White, *90th Division in World War I*, 26–30. Captain Mike Hogg, son of Texas governor James S. Hogg, served with the 360th Infantry and wrote home in a letter: "The class of men that we are getting is better than that of the regular army, however, they are not very literate. For instance, there are ten men in my company who cannot read nor write, and the average grade is about the fifth." See Virginia Bernhard (ed.), "A Texan in the Trenches: Mike Hogg's World War I Letters," *Southwestern Historical Quarterly* 117 (July 2013), 54.

[39] *Wichita Daily Times*, Apr. 15, June 13, 15, 17, 21, 29, 1917; *Quanah Tribune Chief*, June 14, 1917; Memorandum from Noah Roark, to A. W. Bloor, Nov. 8, 1917, HQ Corr. And Doc File 10-499 (National Archives); *San Antonio Express*, Aug, 17, 1917; White, *90th Division in World War I*, 38.

[40] *New York Times*, Nov. 11, Dec. 25, 30, 1917, Feb. 15, 16, 24, March 14, May 26, 1918.

[41] White, *Panthers to Arrowheads*, 58–59; *Dallas Morning News*, Dec. 3–6, 30,

1917; *New York Times*, Dec. 19, 1917. One issue that complicated an improvement of sanitary conditions at Camp Bowie was General Greble's visit to the Western Front from September–November 1917, see *New York Times*, Feb. 16, 1918.

[42] *New York Times*, Dec. 1, 29, 1917; White, *90th Division in the World War*, 32.

[43] White, *Panthers to Arrowheads*, 60–61; White, *90th Division in World War I*, 72; *New York Times*, Jan. 27, 1918.

[44] *Dallas Morning News*, Feb. 2, 1918; Ball, *They Called Them Soldier Boys*; White, *90th Division in World War I*, 48.

[45] White, *Panthers to Arrowheads*, 82–83; White, *90th Division in World War I*, 44–45; *Dallas Morning News*, Nov. 22, 1917.

[46] White, *Panthers to Arrowheads*, 83, 89; White, *90th Division in World War I*, 33–36, 46; *Order of Battle of the United States Land Forces in the World War*, II, 410–411; *New York Times*, March 13, 1918.

[47] As an example, on July 13, 1918, when the 36th Division was on its way to New York, the U.S. Army moved 41,000 soldiers by rail on 77 special trains.

[48] White, *Panthers to Arrowheads*, 91; Archibald Stephen Hart, *Company K of Yesterday* (New York: Vantage, 1969), 40–41.

## Chapter 6

[1] *New York Times*, June 11, 24, 27, 1918; Wooster, *Texas and Texans in the Great War*, 126. While the names of Texans who fought overseas prior to the arrival of the Thirty-Sixth and Ninetieth Divisions are too numerous to mention, several of the more well-known included Carl Brannen, Warren Jackson, and Herbert Dunlavy, all of whom served with the Sixth Marines. In addition, the writer-artist John W. Thomason Jr. served with the Fifth Marines at Belleau Wood and Blanc Mont. See Wooster, *Texas and Texans in the Great War*, 128–129.

[2] *Wichita Daily Times*, Aug. 21, 29, 1918; *Wise County Messenger*, Aug. 23, Sep. 20, Oct. 18, 1918; Hart, *Company K of Yesterday*, 43–44; William Deming Hornaday, "Transcripts of World War I Letters and Personal Accounts" (24 vols., typescript), X, 65, William Deming Hornaday Collection (Archives Division, Texas State Library, Austin); John J. Pershing, *My Experiences in the First World War* (2 vols., 1931; reprint, New York: Da Capo, 1995), II, 201; *New York Times*, Sep. 24, 1917.

[3] White, *90th Division in World War I*, 85–86.

[4] Ibid.

[5] Ibid., 86–87.

[6] Ibid., 91–95.

[7] Ibid., 97–98; Bernhard, "A Texan in the Trenches," 63.

[8] White, *90th Division in World War I*, 103–104, 109–110.

[9] Ibid., 86, 112–114.

[10] *Order of Battle of the United States Land Forces in the World War*, II, 415; White, *90th Division in World War I*, 86, 112–114.

[11] *Order of Battle of the United States Land Forces in the World War*, II, 415; White, *90th Division in World War I*, 117–120, 121–127, 134, 148.

[12] White, *90th Division in World War I*, 152, 156.

[13] Barnes, *History of the 142nd Infantry of the Thirty-Sixth Division*, 27; White, *Panthers to Arrowheads*, 105; John Lejeune, *Reminiscences of a Marine* (Philadelphia: Dorrance and Company, 1930), 360–361.

[14] Edwin Hutchings would be killed in the fighting around Saint-Etienne.

[15] White, *Panthers to Arrowheads*, 107–108. A *New York Times* article stated

the following pertaining to the return of Hutchings: "The return to this country of Brig. Gen. Henry Hutchins [sic], formerly with the Texas National Guard troops in France, was announced today by General [Peyton] March, who said that General Pershing had asked permission to send this officer home. The reason for the transfer was not announced. General March added that orders for General Hutchins's discharge from the service had not yet been issued." *New York Times*, Oct. 6, 1918.

[16] White, *Panthers to Arrowheads*, 107–109; Barnes, *History of the 142nd Infantry of the Thirty-Sixth Division*, 342–346; *Wise County Messenger*, Oct. 4, 25, 1918; Ball, "Over the Top: Denton County Soldiers in the Great War, 1917–1918," *Southwestern Historical Quarterly* 114 (October 2010): 137–150.

[17] Ben H. Chastaine, *Story of the Thirty-Sixth: The Experiences of the Thirty-Sixth Division in the World War* (Oklahoma City: Harlow, 1920), 57; White, *Panthers to Arrowheads*, 116.

[18] Lejeune, *Reminiscences of a Marine*, 360–361.

[19] Historical Branch, War Plans Division, General Staff, *Blanc Mont (Meuse-Argonne-Champagne)* (Washington, D.C.: Government Printing Office, 1922); George C. Marshall, *Infantry in Battle* (2nd ed.; Richmond, Va.: Garrett and Massie, 1939), iv, 164; *Wichita Daily Times*, Oct. 20, 1918; *New York Times*, Oct. 20, 1918.

[20] "Forest Farm Engagement, Operations Report," Oct. 27, 1918, Box 14, 142nd Infantry, Thirty-Sixth Division, RG 120 (National Archives).

[21] Personnel Experiences Folder, Lillard, 3, Box 14, 142nd Infantry, Thirty-Sixth Division, RG 120 (National Archives).

[22] "Memorandum from C.O. 142nd Infantry to C.O. 36th Division, Subject: Transmitting Messages in Choctaw," Jan. 23, 1919, Box 14, 142nd Infantry, Thirty-Sixth Division, RG 120 (National Archives).

[23] Ibid.

[24] Ibid.

[25] White, *90th Division in World War I*, 115, 210–211.

[26] Ibid., 194–198.

[27] Chastaine, *Story of the Thirty-Sixth*, 242–243, 246–247; Barnes, *History of the 142nd Infantry of the Thirty-Sixth Division*, 41–42, 142–143; *New York Times*, Nov. 13, 1918.

[28] White, *90th Division in World War I*, 163.

[29] *New York Times*, Dec. 2, 1918; *Order of Battle of the United States Land Forces in the World War*, II, 415; White, *90th Division in World War I*, 164. White provides a detailed discussion of the Ninetieth Division in Germany. See White, *90th Division in World War I*, 168–173 and 176–178.

[30] Barnes, *History of the 142nd Infantry of the Thirty-Sixth Division*, 46–47; Hornaday, "Transcripts" (24 vols., typescript), V, 85–86; *Blum Bulletin*, Jan. 9, 1919; Chastaine, *Story of the Thirty-Sixth*, 260.

[31] Barnes, *History of the 142nd Infantry of the Thirty-Sixth Division*, 47; Chastaine, *Story of the Thirty-Sixth*, 248; Hornaday, "Transcripts" (24 vols., typescript), II, 345, and IX, 258.

[32] Hornaday, "Transcripts" (24 vols., typescript), I, 298; III, 250–252; V, 347, IV, 253–255; *Abilene Reporter*, Feb. 5, 1919.

[33] Chastaine, *Story of the Thirty-Sixth*, 259–261; White, *90th Division in World War I*, 179–180. The Ninetieth Division also played and lost to the Eighty-Ninth Division.

[34] White, *90th Division in World War I*, 161–163. Although most frequently referred to as the "Alamo Division," the Ninetieth was also referred to as the "Rat-

tlesnake Division," the "Outlaw Division," and perhaps most appropriately, as the "Tough 'Ombres," which was apparently one way that General Allen referred to his troops privately.

[35] White, *90th Division in World War I*, 163.

[36] *New York Times*, Oct. 3, 4, 10, 1918; White, *90th Division in World War I*, 187; Wooster, *Texas and Texans in the Great War*, 155; Ana Martínez-Catsam, "Desolate Streets: The Spanish Influenza in San Antonio," *Southwestern Historical Quarterly* 116 (January 2013): 287–303.

[37] White, *90th Division in World War I*, 201; *Order of Battle of the United States Land Forces in the World War*, II, 417; Ball, *They Called Them Soldier Boys*, 406.

[38] White, *90th Division in World War I*, 200–208.

[39] Ibid., 201; *Order of Battle of the United States Land Forces in the World War*, II, 417; Ball, *They Called Them Soldier Boys*, 406.

## *Chapter 7*

[1] World War I Medal of Honor Recipients, U.S. Army Center of Military History, <history.army.mil/moh/worldwari.html> [Accessed Nov. 8, 2016].

[2] Ibid.

[3] Ibid.; Alexander Mendoza, "Tejanos at War: A History of Mexican Texans in America's Wars," in Mendoza and Grear, *Texans and War*, 50.

[4] World War I Medal of Honor Recipients, U.S. Army Center of Military History, <history.army.mil/moh/worldwari.html> [Accessed Nov. 8, 2016]; Wooster, *Texas and Texans in the Great War*, 127.

[5] World War I Medal of Honor Recipients, U.S. Army Center of Military History, <history.army.mil/moh/worldwari.html> [Accessed Nov. 8, 2016].

[6] White, *The 90th Division in World War I*, 191; Wooster, *Texas and Texans in the Great War*, 126, 131; Mendoza, "Tejanos at War," 38.

[7] Hazlewood, "Camp Logan"; Smyrl, "Camp MacArthur."

[8] Kirkland, "Texas Women at War," 73; *New York Times*, June 25, 1917.

[9] Other Texans who served in Siberia included former University of Texas athletic star Kearie Lee Berry, El Paso correspondent Peggy Hull, and Dr. Joseph Kopecky, who ran a hospital during the Siberian Expedition. See Wooster, *Texas and Texans in the Great War*, 152.

[10] *New York Times*, June 29, 1918; Wooster, *Texas and Texans in the Great War*, 118–119, 131–132.

[11] "Biography of General Ira C. Eaker," USAF Public Affairs, <http://www.af.mil/AboutUs/Biographies/Display/tabid/225/Article/107172/general-ira-c-eaker.aspx> [Accessed Nov. 10, 2016]. Other Texans who served in World War I and reached general officer rank in World War II included Yantis Taylor, Leonard Weddington, William O. Ryan, George H. Beverly, Warren R. Carter, Charles C. Chauncey, John M. Clark, Davenport Johnson, Howard C. Davidson, Ralph P. Cousins, William E. Farthing, and Ray G. Harris.

[12] *New York Times*, June 29, 1918. Lieutenant Ralph H. Cameron was another example. During the war, Cameron served with the U.S. Army Corps of Engineers. As an architect in San Antonio, he left his mark on the city. Appointed as the official architect of the San Antonio School Board in 1913, he helped design Brackenridge High School, Main Avenue High School, Robert E. Lee School, McKinley School, West End School, the Maverick Clarke Building, and numerous residences. He also designed buildings in other towns, such as Floresville City Hall and Masonic

Temples in Lufkin, Uvalde, and Brady. During the war, Cameron served with the Army Corps of Engineers. See *San Antonio Express*, Aug. 17, 1917; White, *The 90th Division in World War I*, 104, 126. See also Harold J. Meyer, *Hanging Sam: A Military Biography of General Samuel T. Williams* (Denton: University of North Texas Press, 1990) and Henry C. Dethloff with John A. Adams Jr., *Texas Aggies Go to War in Service of Their Country* (College Station: Texas A&M University Press, 2006), 29–62.

[13] Wooster, *Texas and Texans in the Great War*, 165–166.

[14] Wooster, *Texas and Texans in the Great War*, 167.

[15] Alwyn Barr, "The Influence of War and Military Service on African Texans," in Mendoza and Grear, *Texans and War*, 105–107.

[16] Mendoza, "Tejanos at War," 48–50.

# INDEX